THE
BAKING
BOOK

Linda Collister & Anthony Blake

THE BAKING BOOK

Conran Octopus

TO ALAN, BOBBY AND NICKY

Both metric and imperial quantities
are given in the recipes. Use either all metric or all imperial,
as the two are not interchangeable.

First published 1996 by
Conran Octopus Limited
37 Shelton Street
London WC2H 9HN

Commissioning Editor Louise Simpson
Project Editor Norma MacMillan
Designer Paul Welti
Production Julia Golding

A catalogue record for this book is available from the British Library.

ISBN 1 85029 765 7

Typeset by Peter Howard
Printed in China

Front jacket photograph: Strawberry Mille Feuille
(for recipe see page 146)

CONTENTS

INTRODUCTION

Baking sweet things combines many pleasures: there is creative pride in the making, social satisfaction in the sharing, and sensual delight in the eating. But baking is also a craft, and like other crafts it has its subtleties and secrets. So one of the great joys of writing this book has been learning new techniques and recipes. I have sought out professional bakers to find out how they make their pastry so light and their fillings so succulent, and I have asked home cooks to teach me how to make the tastiest brownies, the most luxurious chocolate cakes, the least resistible cookies.

My recipes make food to share, not to impress. I am not keen on elaborate gâteaux, on layers of complex confection and swirls of rich buttercream. I prefer honest sponge cake that tastes of good butter, fresh eggs and real vanilla; pastry that truly melts in the mouth; bread with real flavour, a good texture and a chewy crust. Like many simple things, these are hard to find nowadays.

Children enjoy working in the kitchen. These two young members of the Meyer family always help their mother, Dee Dee, with the cooking (see also pages 50–51).

INGREDIENTS

Most people who care about their craft are fussy about their materials: me too! For cake making, all ingredients – including the fat and eggs – must be at room temperature before starting. And you need high quality ingredients for a high quality result.

I usually use unsalted butter, which I buy on special offer and freeze. It has a taste all its own, and I would not make a cake or pastry with anything else. My supermarket sells its own label organic flour, and I rely on Mike Thurlow at Letheringsett Mill for superlative bread flour. Both my local baker and health food store sell fresh yeast; it's cheap and freezes well. For baking I prefer unrefined pure cane sugar, including golden caster and golden icing sugar – my supermarket has its own label range. I normally use size 3 (medium) free-range eggs; when my recipes specify large eggs, this means size 2. Nuts should be as fresh as possible; the oils in them start to turn rancid as soon as they are exposed to air, so it is best to store them in the freezer. Finally, there is no substitute for real chocolate. I never use chocolate flavour cake covering or cheap cooking chocolate. Supermarket own label chocolate is usually very good quality and value. See page 118 for more information about chocolate.

EQUIPMENT

For making pastry and cakes, precise measurements are vital – after all, it's chemistry! So accurate scales and a good set of measuring spoons are essential. A teaspoon is 5ml and a tablespoon is 15ml; all should be measured level unless the recipe calls for a rounded or heaped spoon. A clear measuring jug is very useful.

You cannot bake well without a good, controllable oven. This summer I made my best pies ever on a bottled gas stove in an island log cabin, which must prove that ultra-modern, top-of-the-range appliances are not necessarily better than their cheaper, simpler ancestors. An oven thermometer is essential: thermostats are often unreliable, and you need to learn how your own oven behaves – and to trust your knowledge. The cooking instructions given in these recipes are guidelines; your oven handbook and your experience will teach you which shelf works best. Baking times should usually be reduced for fan ovens; again please check your handbook. But I always preheat the oven, despite what the manufacturers say. For getting advice on ovens, see page 190.

An electric mixer makes cake batters and kneads bread doughs efficiently and quickly. Care must be taken not to overbeat mixtures, so consult the handbook for speeds and times.

Hard though this is to admit, I would not make pastry without a food processor – my machine does it better than my hands.

If you do a lot of baking, heavy-duty professional-quality tins and trays are a good investment. They will not buckle or scorch in the oven or rust after washing, and they should last a lifetime. See page 190 for where to get advice and mail-order suppliers.

Non-stick baking parchment, sometimes called Bakewell paper, is particularly useful for lining baking trays when making meringues or delicate biscuits.

A large wire cooling rack is very convenient, though you can also use the rack from a grill pan or an oven shelf.

Airtight containers or tins are handy for storing cakes, biscuits and pastries after they have cooled completely.

Happy baking – and even happier eating!

All over the world, beautifully decorated breads are an important part of seasonal feast day and holiday celebrations. Here, a Bulgarian harvest loaf completes the traditional repast of cheese, wine, fruit and nuts.

CHAPTER ONE

BISCUITS, COOKIES & SMALL CAKES

Chewy chunky American cookies, thin crisp
Continental biscuits, brownies, muffins, rock
cakes, scones — all made by the batch to eat
by the dozen. Simple, quick, irresistible.

SHORTBREAD THINS

Makes about 20
170g (6oz) unsalted butter, at room temperature
85g (3oz) caster sugar
230g (8oz) plain flour
30g (1oz) rice flour, ground rice or cornflour
a little caster sugar for sprinkling

a 6.5cm (2⅝in) fluted round biscuit cutter
several baking trays, lightly greased

A crisp, buttery Shortbread Thin.

The traditional recipe for shortbread is three parts flour to two of butter and one of sugar. Most good shortbread bakers, who are usually Scots, like to replace some of the flour with rice flour, ground rice or cornflour, to give a lighter, shorter and sandier texture. The flavour is largely determined by the type and quality of the butter. Good unsalted butter and lactic butter give superb taste as well as texture; whey butter — made by cheese-makers as a by-product — makes a very light, crisp shortbread; while well-salted blended butter tends to make the shortbread heavy and greasy. Several older Scottish bakers told me they mix their local country butter with white vegetable fat or margarine to get a lighter, shorter, more delicate biscuit. I prefer shortbread thin and crisp; however, the same mixture can be rolled out thicker or simply pressed into a lightly greased shortbread tin or shallow cake tin, to make it anything from 6mm–2.5cm (¼–1in) thick. In this case it is best to score the mixture into sections before baking, to make it easier to remove afterwards.

Beat the butter until soft and creamy, using a wooden spoon or electric mixer. Add the sugar and beat until the mixture is pale and fluffy. Sift the plain flour with the rice flour and mix in. When the mixture comes together, turn it on to a lightly floured work surface and knead lightly and briefly to make a smooth but not sticky dough. (If the dough seems sticky, chill it until firm.)

Roll out the dough 5mm (just under ¼in) thick and cut out rounds using the fluted cutter. Gently knead together the trimmings, then re-roll and cut more rounds. Arrange the rounds slightly apart on the prepared baking trays. Prick the rounds with a fork, and chill for 15 minutes.

Preheat the oven to 180C (350F, Gas 4).

Bake the biscuits in the preheated oven for 12–15 minutes or until just firm and barely coloured. Sprinkle with caster sugar and leave to cool on the trays for a minute or two. When firm enough, transfer to a wire rack to cool completely. Store in an airtight tin, and eat within a week.

VARIATION: CHOCOLATE SHORTBREAD Replace 30g (1oz) of the plain flour with cocoa powder, and sift with the flours. As chocolate shortbread scorches more easily, make it thicker and bake it in a tin.

PREVIOUS PAGE (left to right) Cranberry
Muffins, Brownies, Almond Crescents, Chocolate
Chunk Oat Cookies, Tolcarne Ginger Biscuits.

1 WORK THE PLAIN AND RICE FLOURS INTO
THE CREAMED BUTTER MIXTURE.

2 TRANSFER THE ROUNDS TO A GREASED
BAKING TRAY WITH A PALETTE KNIFE.

MILLIONAIRE'S SHORTBREAD

INGREDIENTS

Makes 24
FILLING:
a 397g (about 14oz) can condensed milk

BASE:
170g (6oz) unsalted butter, at room temperature
85g (3oz) caster sugar
230g (8oz) plain flour
30g (1oz) rice flour, ground rice or cornflour

TOPPING:
170g (6oz) good dark chocolate, chopped
30g (1oz) butter
about 60g (2oz) white chocolate to decorate

a 23cm (9in) square tin, about 5cm (2in) deep,
  greased

Super rich — an extravagance of dark chocolate, caramel and butter shortbread.

To make the caramel filling, put the unopened can of condensed milk in a heavy saucepan and cover with water. Bring to the boil, then simmer without covering the pan for 3½ hours, topping up the water as necessary – the can should always be covered. Cool completely before opening the can. The condensed milk will have turned to a fudgy, dark golden caramel.

Meanwhile, make the shortbread base. Preheat the oven to 180C (350F, Gas 4). Beat the butter until creamy, using a wooden spoon or electric mixer. Add the sugar and beat until the mixture is light and fluffy. Sift the plain flour with the rice flour, add to the butter mixture and knead gently for a few seconds until smooth. Press the dough into the prepared tin to make an even layer. Prick all over with a fork, then bake in the preheated oven for 20–30 minutes or until crisp and golden. Cool completely.

When the shortbread base is cold, spread the cooled caramel filling evenly over the top. Chill until firm – about 1 hour.

WHEN THE LAYER OF CARAMEL IS SET AND FIRM, SPREAD OVER THE DARK CHOCOLATE TOPPING USING A SMALL PALETTE KNIFE.

To finish, gently melt the dark chocolate in a heatproof bowl set over a pan of hot but not boiling water. Remove from the heat and stir in the butter until melted and smooth. Spread the mixture evenly over the caramel and leave to set. Melt the white chocolate in the same way, then use a fork or small spoon to drizzle it over the dark chocolate layer in a zigzag pattern (this can also be done using a greaseproof paper icing bag). Leave until set and firm before cutting into fingers or squares.

VARIATION To make a quick and even richer caramel, melt 170g (6oz) unsalted butter with 170g (6oz) caster sugar in a heavy saucepan (non-stick is best). Add the contents of the can of condensed milk – unboiled – and bring the mixture to the boil. Boil, stirring constantly, until the mixture turns a good golden caramel colour. Pour the hot mixture over the cooled shortbread base, and leave until cold and set before finishing.

GRASMERE SHORTBREAD

This recipe comes from our friend and fellow food writer, Sallie Morris, who describes herself as a Lake District girl, like her mother before her. Sallie says that it was long the tradition in the Grasmere area to give gingerbread, or ginger shortbread, to the children who cut rushes to cover the earthen floor of the local churches. This evolved into an annual rush-bearing ceremony, in August, and those who took part were given a piece of gingerbread stamped with the local Saint's name plus a penny to buy beer. The most famous gingerbread was made by Mrs Sarah Nelson, and it is still sold in her tiny cottage near the church. The recipe is kept under lock and key in the local bank; indeed, the people who now keep the shop had to pay a deposit before they were allowed to see the recipe. There are many theories about the lovely sandy texture of the gingerbread — some claim it contains fine oatmeal, or perhaps wholemeal flour.

This is Sallie's mother's recipe, and was quoted in a book about Sarah Nelson. We think it is more than equal to the original: rich, sandy and nicely 'hot'. The shortbread can be served plain, cut into fingers or squares, or sandwiched together with ginger buttercream.

INGREDIENTS

Cuts into about 24 pieces
340g (12oz) plain flour
1½ teaspoons ground ginger
¾ teaspoon bicarbonate of soda
170g (6oz) slightly salted butter, chilled
170g (6oz) dark or light muscovado sugar, sifted

BUTTERCREAM:
110g (4oz) slightly salted butter, at room temperature
230g (8oz) icing sugar, sifted
1 teaspoon ground ginger
2 teaspoons finely chopped drained stem ginger
2 teaspoons syrup from the jar of stem ginger

a 20.5–22 x 30.5–32cm (8–8¾ x 12–12½in) Swiss roll tin, greased

ABOVE You should not miss the famous Sarah Nelson gingerbread shop on a visit to Grasmere.

RIGHT The view across Lake Windermere to Grasmere.

14

SALLIE PRESSES MOST OF THE SHORTBREAD MIXTURE INTO THE PREPARED TIN (ABOVE RIGHT) AND THEN SCATTERS THE REST EVENLY OVER THE SURFACE (TOP). SHE SANDWICHES PAIRS OF BAKED SHORTBREAD FINGERS WITH GINGER CREAM (ABOVE).

Preheat the oven to 180C (350F, Gas 4).

Sift the flour, ginger and bicarbonate of soda into a mixing bowl. Cut the butter into small pieces, add to the flour and rub in using the tips of your fingers. When the mixture looks like fine sand, stir in the sugar.

Put three-quarters of the mixture into the prepared tin and press down to make an even layer. Scatter the rest of the mixture evenly over the surface to make a crumbly topping. Use the edge of a ruler or knife to mark into fingers or squares.

Bake in the preheated oven for 35–40 minutes or until pale golden. Cool slightly, then cut into fingers or squares along the marked lines. Leave in the tin until completely cold.

To make the buttercream, beat the butter until creamy using a wooden spoon. Gradually add the icing sugar and ground ginger, beating well, then mix in the chopped stem ginger and syrup to make a spreadable cream. Use to sandwich together pairs of shortbread fingers or squares. Once assembled, eat within 3 days.

TOLCARNE GINGER BISCUITS

INGREDIENTS

Makes 30

340g (12oz) self-raising flour

200g (7oz) golden caster sugar

1 tablespoon ground ginger

1 teaspoon bicarbonate of soda

110g (4oz) unsalted butter

85g (3oz) golden syrup

1 egg, beaten

2 pieces of stem ginger, drained of syrup, about 40g
   (1½oz), finely chopped (optional)

several baking trays, greased

My favourite biscuits — crisp and very gingery. The recipe came from my grandmother, who learnt to bake at school a hundred years ago. Sometimes I add a teaspoon or two of chopped stem ginger — the kind preserved in syrup — when I add the egg.

Preheat the oven to 170C (325F, Gas 3).

Put all the dry ingredients into a mixing bowl and stir until thoroughly combined. Gently melt the butter with the golden syrup. Pour on to the dry ingredients, then add the egg and chopped ginger and mix well with a wooden spoon to make a dough.

Using your hands, roll walnut-sized pieces of the dough into balls — you should have about 30. Place well apart on the prepared baking trays, then slightly flatten each ball with your fingers. Bake in the preheated oven for 15–20 minutes or until crisp and golden. Leave to cool on the trays for a minute before lifting on to a wire rack to cool completely. Store in an airtight tin, and eat within a week.

PRESS EACH BALL OF DOUGH TO FLATTEN IT SLIGHTLY; THIS HELPS THE BISCUIT TO SPREAD AND BAKE EVENLY IN THE OVEN.

LEFT A charming Devon cottage, worthy of a picture postcard.

A selection of freshly baked treats (clockwise from the top): Tolcarne Ginger Biscuits, Shortbread Thins, Chocolate Chunk Oat Cookies, Millionaire's Shortbread.

SWEDISH PEPPER COOKIES

INGREDIENTS

Makes about 60
300g (10½oz) caster sugar
230g (8oz) unsalted butter, at room temperature
1 tablespoon honey
1 egg, beaten
280g (10oz) plain flour
½ teaspoon salt
1 teaspoon ground ginger
1 teaspoon ground cloves
extra caster sugar for flattening

several baking trays, greased

These cookies were baked for us by Rosemary Underdahl, when we visited her in Maine. The recipe comes from her mother-in-law. Although Rosemary's husband was born and raised in Minnesota, his Swedish and Norwegian origins emerge in these, his favourite cookies. Rosemary trained as a teacher — indeed, she had my little ones under control and eager to please within minutes. She's a natural cook and baker, and is always busy catering for special events and fund-raising galas where her eye-catching and delicate Scandinavian dishes are in demand.

The recipe doesn't actually contain pepper, but the cookies certainly taste spicy. The recipe makes a big batch of cookies — if more convenient, you can bake one of the three portions and keep the other two in the fridge or freezer to bake another time.

Beat the sugar with the butter until pale and fluffy, using a wooden spoon, electric mixer or food processor. Beat in the honey and the egg. Sift the flour with the salt, ground ginger and ground cloves, then work into the mixture to make a firm dough.

Divide the dough into three. Shape each portion into a disc and wrap tightly in greaseproof paper. Chill until firm — about 2 hours. The dough can also be frozen for up to a month or kept in the fridge for up to 5 days, ready to be shaped for baking.

When ready to bake, preheat the oven to 190C (375F, Gas 5). Roll marble-size pieces of dough into balls and place them well apart on the prepared baking trays. Dip the base of a glass in cold water and then into a dish of caster sugar; press it gently on top of each ball to flatten it into a wafer-thin disc. Re-sugar the glass frequently, when it starts to stick.

Bake for 7–10 minutes or until barely coloured and firm. Set each baking tray on a wire rack to cool for a minute or so, until the cookies are firm enough to lift off on to a cold baking tray to cool completely. Store in an airtight tin, and eat within 4 days.

1 WORKING QUICKLY, ROSEMARY ROLLS THE WELL-CHILLED DOUGH INTO SMOOTH BALLS THE SIZE OF LARGE MARBLES.

2 SHE FLATTENS THE BALLS USING THE BASE OF A GLASS DIPPED IN SUGAR (THE SUGAR PREVENTS THE DOUGH STICKING).

SWEDISH COCONUT COOKIES

Makes about 60

110g (4oz) unsalted butter, at room temperature

110g (4oz) white vegetable fat, at room
   temperature

100g (3¹/₂oz) caster sugar

230g (8oz) plain flour

¹/₂ teaspoon bicarbonate of soda

¹/₂ teaspoon baking powder

¹/₂ teaspoon pure vanilla essence

50g (1³/₄oz) shredded coconut or desiccated coconut

several baking trays, greased

Right ROSEMARY CUTS THE ROLL OF
THOROUGHLY CHILLED DOUGH INTO
WAFER-THIN SLICES.

BELOW My nephew Lucas is a big fan of
Rosemary's cookies.

VARIATION: ALMOND COOKIES
Add 40g (1¹/₂oz) finely chopped
almonds with the coconut.

This recipe also comes from Rosemary Underdahl's mother-in-law, and is very popular with her daughters, Caitlin and Hannah. Rosemary likes the contrast between American and Scandinavian cookies: the former are large, chewy and packed with ingredients; the latter are thin, small and crisp.

Beat the fats together until evenly blended, using a wooden spoon or electric mixer. Add the sugar and beat again until the mixture is light and fluffy. Sift the flour with the bicarbonate of soda and baking powder, then add to the mixture with the vanilla and coconut. Work the mixture with your hand until it comes together to make a firm dough.

Divide the dough in half and form each portion into a sausage-like roll with your hands – the roll should be about 6cm (2³/₈in) in diameter. Wrap the rolls of dough in greaseproof paper and chill overnight. The dough can be kept in the fridge for up to 5 days or frozen for up to a month, so you can bake one portion and keep the other.

When ready to bake, preheat the oven to 180C (350F, Gas 4). Using a very sharp knife dipped in hot water, cut very thin slices from the roll of dough – no thicker than 2mm (about ¹/₁₆in) if possible. Rosemary says you shouldn't worry if the slices tear or fall apart; just push them together as you arrange them on the prepared baking tray, or cut thicker slices.

Bake in the preheated oven for 6–8 minutes or until very pale gold and just lightly brown on the edges – you need to watch the cookies carefully as they can brown very quickly. Set each tray on a wire rack and leave the cookies to firm up for a minute or two, then lift the cookies carefully on to a cold baking tray to cool. Store in an airtight tin, and eat within 5 days.

GERMAN CHRISTMAS SPICE BISCUITS

Makes about 24
170g (6oz) plain flour
1½ teaspoons ground ginger
½ teaspoon ground cinnamon
½ teaspoon ground mixed spice
60g (2oz) unsalted butter, chilled and diced
85g (3oz) golden caster sugar
2 tablespoons golden syrup
2 tablespoons milk
1 egg yolk

TO DECORATE:
170g (6oz) icing sugar, sifted
1 egg white

biscuit cutters – star, Christmas tree, bell, Santa,
   holly leaf etc
several baking trays, greased
a greaseproof paper icing bag or a small polythene
   bag
thin ribbon

You can shape these crisp, spicy biscuits into stars, Christmas trees, bells or Santas. Then decorate them and thread them on to thin red ribbon to hang on Christmas trees or in windows.

Preheat the oven to 190C (375F, Gas 5).

Sift the flour, ginger, cinnamon and mixed spice into a mixing bowl. Add the diced butter and rub into the dry ingredients using the tips of your fingers, to give fine crumbs. Stir in the sugar. Mix the golden syrup with the milk and egg yolk, add to the bowl and mix with the dry ingredients to make a soft dough.

Turn the dough on to a floured work surface and knead gently for a few seconds until smooth. Roll out 3–6mm (⅛–¼in) thick, then cut out shapes with the biscuit cutters. Using a skewer or cocktail stick, make a hole at the top of each shape large enough to thread a ribbon through. Arrange the biscuits on the prepared baking trays and chill for 10 minutes.

Bake for 10–12 minutes or until golden. Leave on the trays to cool slightly, then, when the biscuits are firm enough, transfer them to a wire rack to cool completely.

To decorate, gradually beat the sifted icing sugar into the egg white to make a smooth icing of piping consistency. Put into the paper icing bag or polythene bag and snip off the point. Pipe a decorative edge on the biscuits, or pipe wavy patterns, names, messages or whatever you fancy. Leave to set, then thread on ribbons for hanging.

ABOVE The Nürnberg Christmas market.

RIGHT During Advent the Albrecht Dürer stübe restaurant in Nürnberg is lavishly decorated.

OPPOSITE The festive window at the Albrecht Dürer stübe, with decorated spice biscuits and traditional ornaments hung on thin ribbons from copper piping.

RIGHT Chocolate Madeleines, made with good dark chocolate and cocoa powder.

CHOCOLATE MADELEINES

INGREDIENTS

Makes 30
140g (5oz) unsalted butter
85g (3oz) good dark chocolate, chopped
140g (5oz) plain flour
2 tablespoons cocoa powder
a pinch of salt
4 eggs
140g (5oz) caster sugar
icing sugar for sprinkling

madeleine moulds, well buttered (see recipe)

As Marcel Proust dipped a madeleine into his tilleul, all his memories of childhood flooded back, and he began his search for lost time. If he had been tasting chocolate madeleines instead, the world's longest novel might never have been written – or it might have been even longer, for these are even more of a delight than the traditional lemon-flavoured madeleines.

The chocolate version is made by adding melted chocolate and replacing some of the flour with cocoa. Madeleines are traditionally baked in shallow shell-shaped moulds (look out for the non-stick type), which are sold in specialist shops, but you can also use well-greased bun tins.

Preheat the oven to 190C (375F, Gas 5).

With a pastry brush, give the moulds a thin coating of melted butter. Chill or freeze until firm, then add a second coat of butter.

To make the madeleines, put the butter and chocolate in a heatproof bowl set over a pan of hot but not boiling water and melt gently. Remove the bowl from the pan and stir until the mixture is smooth. Leave to cool slightly while preparing the other ingredients. Sift the flour twice with the cocoa and salt. Whisk the eggs with the sugar using an electric mixer, until the mixture becomes pale and very thick – when the whisk is lifted out, the mixture should make a ribbon-like trail on the surface. Using a large metal spoon, fold the flour mixture into the egg mixture in three batches, then carefully fold in the chocolate mixture until thoroughly combined – the mixture will lose a little bulk.

Spoon a heaped teaspoon or so of the mixture into each madeleine mould – it should be about two-thirds full. Bake for 10–12 minutes or until just firm to the touch. Cool in the moulds for a minute, then gently loosen each madeleine with a round-bladed knife and turn out on to a wire rack to cool completely. Serve dusted with icing sugar. Store in an airtight tin, and eat within a week.

VARIATION: TRADITIONAL MADELEINES FLAVOURED WITH LEMON
Melt 140g (5oz) unsalted butter and cool slightly. Sift 155g (5½oz) plain flour with a pinch of salt, and whisk 4 eggs with 140g (5oz) caster sugar as above. Fold the flour into the egg mixture, together with the grated rind of 1 unwaxed lemon, then fold in the butter. Bake and cool as above.

BRIGITTE'S ALMOND SQUARES

Brigitte Friis, who comes from Berlin, is a marvellous cook. This is one of her triumphs — a German confection of thin pastry covered with a sticky combination of honey and almonds.

To make the pastry base, sift the flour into a mixing bowl or food processor bowl. Add the diced butter and rub in using your fingertips, or process, until the mixture looks like breadcrumbs. Stir in the sugar. Add the egg yolk and vanilla and work with your hands, or process, to make a smooth shortbread-like dough.

Press the dough into the prepared tin in an even layer, then prick all over with a fork. Chill for 10–15 minutes or until firm.

Preheat the oven to 190C (375F, Gas 5).

Bake the pastry base for about 10 minutes or until firm and golden.

For the topping, put the almonds, butter, sugar and honey into a wide heavy pan — Brigitte uses a non-stick frying pan — and cook over low heat, stirring constantly, until the mixture is a pale straw gold. Stir in the cream and cook for a few more seconds, then pour over the pastry base and spread in an even layer. Bake for about 10 minutes or until the topping is a deep golden brown.

Leave to cool in the tin, then cut into small squares. Store in an airtight tin, and eat within 5 days.

INGREDIENTS

Makes 40 small squares
PASTRY:
170g (6oz) plain flour
110g (4oz) unsalted butter, chilled and diced
30g (1oz) caster sugar
1 egg yolk
a few drops of pure vanilla essence

TOPPING:
170g (6oz) flaked almonds
85g (3oz) unsalted butter
40g (1½oz) golden caster sugar
40g (1½oz) set honey
2 tablespoons single or double cream

a 20.5–22 x 30.5–32cm (8–8¾ x
   12–12½in) Swiss roll tin, or baking
   tray with an edge, greased

CHOCOLATE MACAROONS

INGREDIENTS

Makes 8 filled macaroons
MACAROONS:
100g (3¹/₂oz) good dark chocolate, chopped
2 egg whites
140g (5oz) unblanched almonds, very finely
 ground
140g (5oz) caster sugar

FILLING:
110g (4oz) good dark chocolate, chopped
100ml (3¹/₂fl oz) double cream or crème fraîche

a baking tray, lined with non-stick baking
 parchment

One of my favourite pastry shops is Ladurée in the Rue Royale in Paris. It is the pâtisserie of your dreams: gilt and marble fittings, velvet banquettes, cakes displayed like Cartier necklaces, chic dowagers perched on tiny chairs and attended by pretty young men or immaculate, lace-trimmed grandchildren. Ladurée's cakes are legendary, and best of all are their chocolate macaroons — sheer heaven with chocolat chaud on a cold day.

This is my version of their recipe. It is best made with top quality dark chocolate — one that contains over 70% cocoa solids. Unblanched almonds are the ones that still have the thin papery brown skin. If you can't find them already ground, you can grind them with the sugar in a food processor or blender.

Preheat the oven to 135C (275F, Gas 1).

Put the chocolate in a heatproof bowl set over a pan of hot but not boiling water and melt very gently; remove from the heat and stir until smooth. Using an electric mixer or whisk, whisk the egg whites until they form soft peaks. Gradually whisk in the almonds combined with the sugar. Gently fold in the melted chocolate using a metal spoon.

Put a heaped tablespoon of the mixture on the prepared baking tray and spread to form a round about 7.5cm (3in) in diameter. Repeat with the rest of the mixture to give 16 rounds. Bake for 1 hour or until firm. Cool slightly on the baking tray, then transfer to a wire rack to cool completely.

To make the mousse filling, put the chopped chocolate in a small heavy pan with the cream and heat gently, stirring occasionally, until melted. Remove from the heat and leave until cool, then beat well with a wooden spoon until thick and fluffy. Chill until firm.

Sandwich pairs of macaroons together with the mousse filling, spreading it generously. Leave for about an hour before serving.

I like these macaroons best when they are a couple of days old, and they have become wonderfully sticky.

CHOCOLATE CHUNK OAT COOKIES

INGREDIENTS

Makes about 24

170g (6oz) good dark chocolate
110g (4oz) unsalted butter, at room temperature
85g (3oz) light muscovado sugar
1 egg, beaten
60g (2oz) self-raising flour
1/2 teaspoon baking powder
110g (4oz) rolled oats
1/2 teaspoon pure vanilla essence

several baking trays, greased

Top quality dark chocolate, chopped into large pieces, makes the best chocolate chip cookies — the taste is unrivalled because good chocolate, with over 70% cocoa solids, contains far less sugar than commercial chocolate chips or dots. As you bite into a thick chunk of rich chocolate you realise that bought cookies can never compete with home-made.

Preheat the oven to 180C (350F, Gas 4).

Using a large sharp knife, coarsely chop the chocolate; set aside. Beat the butter until creamy using a wooden spoon or electric mixer. Add the sugar and beat until light and fluffy. Gradually beat in the egg and continue beating for 1 minute. Sift the flour with the baking powder and stir into the mixture with the oats and vanilla. When thoroughly combined, add the chocolate and mix well.

Place heaped teaspoons of the mixture, well spaced apart, on the prepared baking trays. Lightly flatten the mounds, then bake in the preheated oven for 12–15 minutes or until golden and just firm. Leave to cool on the trays for a minute, then transfer to a wire rack to cool completely. Store in an airtight tin, and eat within a week.

VARIATION: CHOCOLATE NUT COOKIES Omit the oats, increase the flour by 30g (1oz), and add 90g (3oz) chopped hazelnuts.

USE A HEAVY, SHARP KNIFE TO CHOP THE CHOCOLATE INTO LARGE CHUNKS.

HAZELNUT COOKIES

Makes about 30

70g (2¹/₂oz) hazelnuts

110g (4oz) unsalted butter, at room temperature

¹/₂ teaspoon pure vanilla essence

85g (3oz) light muscovado sugar

60g (2oz) golden caster sugar

1 egg, beaten

280g (10oz) plain flour

1¹/₂ teaspoons baking powder

a pinch of salt

several baking trays

Toasting nuts changes their taste from mild and creamy to an almost caramel, bittersweet richness. These cookies can be made with toasted pecans or untoasted walnuts, but I think hazelnuts give them the best flavour.

Preheat the oven to 180C (350F, Gas 4).

Spread the hazelnuts on an ungreased baking tray and toast in the preheated oven for 10–15 minutes or until they turn a good golden brown and the skin is starting to crack and peel. Gather up the hazelnuts in a clean tea towel so they are held as if in a purse and rub them together to loosen the skins. Chop the skinned nuts coarsely using a large sharp knife or in a food processor.

Beat the butter with the vanilla until creamy, using a wooden spoon or electric mixer. Add the sugars and beat again until light and fluffy. Gradually beat in the egg. Sift the flour with the baking powder and salt, and stir into the mixture with the chopped nuts to make a firm dough.

Turn on to a lightly floured work surface and form into a log shape about 21.5 x 5.5cm (8¹/₂ x 2¹/₄in). Wrap in greaseproof paper or non-stick baking parchment and chill until firm – about 2 hours. The dough can be kept in the fridge for up to a week.

When ready to bake, preheat the oven to 190C (375F, Gas 5). Using a large sharp knife, cut the log into slices about 5mm (just under ¹/₄in) thick. Arrange them slightly apart on greased baking trays and bake for about 15 minutes or until golden and just firm to the touch. Transfer to wire racks to cool.

Store the cookies in an airtight tin, and eat within 5 days.

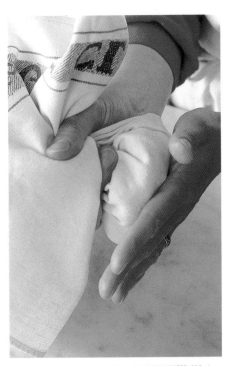 

LEFT (from left to right): Somerset Easter Biscuits, Belgian Spice Biscuits, Hazelnut Cookies.

1 GATHER THE TOASTED HAZELNUTS IN A TEA TOWEL AND RUB THEM TOGETHER.

2 THE FRICTION CREATED BY RUBBING THE NUTS WILL LOOSEN THEIR PAPERY SKINS.

ALMOND CRESCENTS

INGREDIENTS

Makes about 22
110g (4oz) unsalted butter, at room temperature
2-3 drops of pure almond essence (optional)
60g (2oz) icing sugar, sifted
a pinch of salt
85g (3oz) plain flour, sifted
110g (4oz) ground almonds
extra icing sugar for dredging

several baking trays, greased

ABOVE Almond trees in blossom.

OPPOSITE Sugar-dredged Almond Crescents are
well partnered by a glass of sweet wine.

Every Christmas, a Czech friend used to make a wonderful big box of these snow-white biscuits for my mother but wouldn't divulge the recipe. I've since enjoyed them at holiday time in the houses of Polish, German and Dutch friends, and my American mother-in-law says the recipe is an old Jewish one. From clues dropped here and there I've gradually worked out the proportions — the method is very simple. I like to serve the biscuits with fruit desserts such as oranges in caramel, poached pears, or strawberries and cream, as well as with coffee.

Preheat the oven to 170C (325F, Gas 3).

Using a wooden spoon or electric mixer, beat the butter with the almond essence until very light and creamy. Add the sugar and mix slowly until combined, then beat until fluffy. Add the remaining ingredients and mix thoroughly using a wooden spoon. Knead lightly to bring the dough together – it should be firm.

Take a good teaspoon-sized portion of dough and roll it with your hands to make a sausage about 7.5cm (3in) long, then curve to make a crescent. Place on a prepared baking tray. Repeat with the rest of the dough, spacing the crescents well apart. Bake in the preheated oven for 15–18 minutes or until firm. The biscuits should remain pale with only the tips slightly coloured.

Dredge with icing sugar, then leave to cool on the trays for a couple of minutes. Transfer to a wire rack to cool completely. Store in an airtight tin, and eat within a week. The flavour develops if the biscuits are kept for at least a day after baking.

CURVE THE SAUSAGES OF DOUGH INTO NEAT CRESCENT SHAPES USING YOUR FINGERTIPS.

DOUBLE CHOCOLATE PECAN COOKIES

Makes about 28

100g (3¹/₂oz) rolled oats

140g (5oz) plain flour

a pinch of salt

¹/₂ teaspoon baking powder

¹/₂ teaspoon bicarbonate of soda

200g (7oz) good dark chocolate

110g (4oz) unsalted butter, at room temperature

85g (3oz) golden caster sugar

85g (3oz) light muscovado sugar

1 egg, beaten

110g (4oz) pecans, coarsely chopped

several baking trays

Really good chocolate, grated and chopped into large chunks, makes the richest, darkest, most luxurious cookies. I like to add pecans — my favourite nut when cooking with chocolate — but chopped walnuts or a mixture of nuts are also good. To make white chocolate nut cookies, still use the grated dark chocolate, but replace the chopped dark chocolate with an equal quantity of good white chocolate.

Preheat the oven to 190C (375F, Gas 5).

Spread the oats on an ungreased baking tray and toast in the preheated oven, stirring occasionally, for about 15 minutes or until golden. Leave to cool, then put into the food processor with the flour, salt, baking powder and bicarbonate of soda. Process until the mixture has the texture of sand. Finely grate 50g (1³/₄oz) of the chocolate, and chop the remaining 150g (5¹/₄oz) into large chunks.

Beat the butter until creamy, using an electric mixer or wooden spoon. Add the sugars and beat again until light and fluffy. Gradually beat in the egg, then continue beating for 1 minute. Stir in the oat mixture, grated and chopped chocolate, and pecans to make a stiff dough — in cold weather, you may need to use your hands to work it together.

Roll walnut-sized pieces of dough into balls with your hands. Place the balls well spaced apart on greased baking trays and bake for about 12 minutes or until almost firm. Leave to cool on the trays for a minute, then transfer the cookies to a wire rack to cool completely. Store in an airtight tin, and eat within 5 days.

Nuts go rancid quite quickly, so when making Double Chocolate Pecan Cookies use the freshest pecans you can find — just shelled if possible.

SOMERSET EASTER BISCUITS

Makes about 15
110g (4oz) unsalted butter, at room temperature
85g (3oz) golden caster sugar
1 egg yolk
200g (7oz) plain flour
a pinch of salt
a good pinch of baking powder
a good pinch of grated nutmeg
$^1/_2$ teaspoon ground mixed spice
$^1/_2$ teaspoon ground cinnamon
60g (2oz) raisins or currants
1 teaspoon finely chopped mixed candied peel

TO FINISH:
1 egg white, lightly beaten
caster sugar for sprinkling

a 6.5cm (2$^5/_8$in) fluted round biscuit cutter
several baking trays, greased

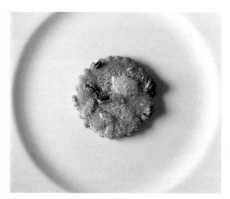

ABOVE A spicy Somerset Easter Biscuit, with its
sugary glaze.

TOP RIGHT The River Parrot on Sedgemoor in
Somerset.

I spent many a happy Easter on a farm in Somerset, so I always associate these short, slightly spicy biscuits with the West Country. My friend Michael Sealey has a passion for afternoon tea, and serves these biscuits in stacks of three tied with yellow ribbon. He likes to use currants, but I prefer raisins. The choice is yours.

Preheat the oven to 200C (400F, Gas 6).
Beat the butter until creamy, using a wooden spoon or electric mixer. Add the sugar and beat until the mixture is light and fluffy. Add the egg yolk and beat for a further minute. Sift the flour with the salt, baking powder, nutmeg, mixed spice and cinnamon. Add to the butter mixture and stir until thoroughly combined. Add the fruit and peel and mix well with your hands. If the dough seems very stiff or dry and doesn't come together, add a tablespoon of milk.
Turn the dough on to a floured work surface and knead lightly for a few seconds. Roll out about 5mm (slightly less than $^1/_4$in) thick. Cut out rounds with the fluted biscuit cutter, then re-roll the trimmings and cut out more rounds. Arrange the biscuit rounds, spaced a little apart, on the prepared baking trays.
Bake in the preheated oven for 10 minutes or until pale golden and firm. Remove from the oven. Lightly brush each biscuit with egg white, then sprinkle with a little caster sugar. Return the biscuits to the oven and bake for a further 3–5 minutes or until the tops turn golden and crunchy. Transfer to a wire rack to cool.
Store the biscuits in an airtight tin, and eat within 5 days.

BELGIAN SPICE BISCUITS

INGREDIENTS

Makes about 40
200g (7oz) plain flour
$^1/_2$ teaspoon ground ginger
$^1/_2$ teaspoon ground cinnamon
$^1/_2$ teaspoon ground mixed spice
$^1/_2$ teaspoon baking powder
110g (4oz) unsalted butter, chilled and diced
85g (3oz) light muscovado sugar
about 45g (1$^1/_2$oz) split (halved) almonds

several baking trays, lined with non-stick baking
  parchment

These thin, crisp, fragile biscuits are of the 'ice-box' variety — the dough is shaped into a brick, wrapped, chilled and then sliced when ready to bake. I like them best with a cup of coffee after dinner, but they are a treat at any time of day.

Sift the flour with the ginger, cinnamon, mixed spice and baking powder. Tip into a food processor, add the diced butter and process until the mixture looks like fine crumbs. Add the sugar and process until the mixture comes together to make a firm dough — in cold weather you may have to knead the dough a little by hand. The dough can also be made by rubbing the fat into the flour mixture with your fingers, then stirring in the sugar, and finally kneading the dough together.

Turn the dough on to a work surface and shape it into a brick about 17.5 x 7.5 x 3cm (7 x 3 x 1$^1/_4$in). Wrap in greaseproof paper and chill until firm — at least 2 hours. The dough can be kept in the fridge for up to 5 days and then baked when convenient.

When ready to bake, preheat the oven to 200C (400F, Gas 6). Using a large sharp knife, cut the dough into very thin slices — you should have about 40. Arrange slightly apart on the prepared baking trays and press an almond half into the middle of each slice. Bake for 5–7 minutes or until golden. Cool on the trays for a minute, then transfer to a wire rack to cool completely. Store in an airtight tin, and eat within 4 days.

Crisp Belgian Spice Biscuits can be freshly baked whenever you want them.

THE DOUGH MUST BE VERY FIRM SO THAT IT CAN BE CUT INTO WAFER-THIN SLICES.

PLAIN SCONES

INGREDIENTS

Makes 8
230g (8oz) self-raising flour
a pinch of salt
40g (1¹/₂oz) golden caster sugar
40g (1¹/₂oz) unsalted butter, chilled and diced
1 egg, made up to 140ml (5fl oz) with milk
extra flour for rolling out

a 6cm (2³/₈in) fluted round biscuit cutter
a baking tray, greased

I'm quite proud of my scones, if only because they got me my first job. Over the last 20 years I've tried every recipe I've come across — ones using soured milk or buttermilk; risen with various combinations of bicarbonate of soda and cream of tartar, or baking powder; made with cream, or with golden syrup, with or without eggs. To get a moist, well-flavoured scone that is light and well risen you need a raising agent or agents — but use too much and you just get a huge scone with a nasty chemical aftertaste. I found it quite difficult to get the proportions to my liking, so I went back to the simplest recipe, using self-raising flour, and got the best results. A light touch is also required here — too much kneading or overworking will develop the gluten in the flour and make the dough elastic, so it becomes tough and hard when baked. Making the dough in the food processor overcomes this to a certain extent — it is also very quick.

I think scones spread thickly with clotted cream and good strawberry jam make the finest afternoon tea yet invented.

Preheat the oven to 220C (425F, Gas 7).

Sift the flour and salt into a bowl, then tip into the bowl of a food processor. Add the sugar and run the machine for a few seconds just to combine the ingredients. Add the diced butter and process until there are no lumps and the mixture looks like sand. Beat the egg with the milk just

until mixed. Slowly pour into the processor through the feed tube while the machine is running; stop pouring and turn off the machine as soon as the mixture forms a rather soft but not sticky ball of dough. If the dough seems dry and stiff, add a little extra milk.

Turn the dough on to a well-floured work surface. If the dough feels sticky and is hard to handle, sprinkle it with a little flour and work this in by gentle kneading; however, try not to work the dough more than necessary. Lightly knead the dough until it forms a rough-looking ball, then using your fingers pat it out 2cm (¾in) thick. Dip the cutter in flour and cut out as many rounds as possible. Gather up the trimmings into a ball, then pat out again and cut more rounds.

Arrange the rounds of dough well apart on the prepared baking tray and bake immediately. They will take 12–15 minutes and should be a good golden brown, risen and firm. Transfer from the baking tray to a wire rack. Eat warm the same day, or split and toast. When completely cold the scones can be frozen for up to a month.

TO MAKE SCONES WITHOUT A PROCESSOR, sift the flour and salt into a bowl, mix in the sugar and add the diced butter. Rub the butter into the dry ingredients using the tips of your fingers. When the mixture resembles fine crumbs, add the egg and milk mixture. Stir in using a round-bladed knife to make a soft dough. Finish as above.

1 PROCESS THE BUTTER WITH THE DRY INGREDIENTS TO A SAND-LIKE TEXTURE.

2 ADD ENOUGH EGG AND MILK TO MAKE A SOFT DOUGH THAT IS NOT STICKY.

3 TURN OUT THE DOUGH ON TO A WELL-FLOURED WORK SURFACE.

4 KNEAD THE DOUGH LIGHTLY TO BLEND THE INGREDIENTS, THEN FORM A BALL.

5 PAT OUT THE DOUGH WITH YOUR FINGERS TO A DISC 2CM (¾IN) THICK.

6 CUT OUT ROUNDS WITH A FLOURED CUTTER AND PLACE ON A BAKING TRAY.

STRAWBERRY SHORTCAKE

INGREDIENTS

Serves 4–5
450g (1lb) ripe strawberries, hulled
1–2 tablespoons caster sugar, to taste
about 85g (3oz) unsalted butter, at room
   temperature, for spreading

SHORTCAKE:
250g (8³/₄oz) self-raising flour
¹/₂ teaspoon baking powder
a large pinch of salt
80g (2³/₄oz) caster sugar
80g (2³/₄oz) unsalted butter, chilled and diced
about 230ml (8fl oz) whipping cream, chilled
a few drops of pure vanilla essence

a 7.5cm (3in) plain round biscuit cutter
a baking tray, greased

When planning my American father-in-law's 70th birthday dinner, I asked him to name his favourite dessert. 'Strawberry Shortcake — but hold the shortcake', was the reply. Will loves strawberries, but finds that too often the shortcake tastes like cardboard. 'It should be warm, rich with butter and cream, but also light and flaky', he says. Eventually I came up with this recipe — and it got the smacked lips of approval. The shortcake is similar to British scones (see previous page), but is made with cream instead of egg and milk, giving a texture and taste somewhere between a scone, shortbread and spongecake. Serve with a jug of thick pouring cream.

Preheat the oven to 220C (425F, Gas 7).
   Thickly slice the strawberries and toss with a little sugar. Put aside.
   Sift the flour, baking powder, salt and sugar into a mixing bowl. Add the diced butter and quickly rub into the dry ingredients with the tips of your fingers until the mixture resembles lumpy crumbs. Add the cream and vanilla and mix with a round-bladed knife until the mixture comes together to form a stiff dough.
   Turn on to a lightly floured work surface, and pat into a brick. Using a rolling pin, roll out the dough to a rectangle 1.2cm (¹/₂in) thick. Fold the dough into three: fold the bottom third of the rectangle up to cover the centre third, then fold the top third down over this, to make three layers. Roll or pat out the dough again until it is 2.5cm (1in) thick. Cut out rounds using the biscuit cutter, then gently knead and re-roll the trimmings to give four or five rounds in all.
   Place the dough rounds on the prepared baking tray and bake in the preheated oven for 10 minutes. Reduce the oven temperature to 180C (350F, Gas 4), and bake for a further 10–15 minutes or until firm and golden. Leave on the tray to cool slightly, then carefully transfer to a wire rack to cool completely.
   When ready to serve, preheat the oven to 180C (350F, Gas 4). Split the shortcakes in half horizontally and butter the cut surfaces. Divide two-thirds of the strawberries among the shortcake bases. Cover with the lids and arrange the rest of the berries on top. Put the assembled shortcakes on a baking tray and heat in the oven for 3–4 minutes or until they are warm and the butter is starting to melt. Eat immediately, with cream.

OPPOSITE Strawberry Shortcake, an all-American favourite.

ARRANGE MOST OF THE STRAWBERRY SLICES ON THE BUTTERED SHORTCAKE BASES.

CRANBERRY MUFFINS

INGREDIENTS

Makes 12

140g (5oz) unbleached plain flour

140g (5oz) stoneground wholemeal bread flour

1 tablespoon baking powder

a large pinch of salt

85g (3oz) golden caster sugar

the grated rind of ½ unwaxed orange

1 egg, size 1, beaten

280ml (10fl oz) whole milk

2 teaspoons orange juice

60ml (2fl oz) soya oil

140g (5oz) fresh or frozen cranberries – use
    straight from freezer

a 12-hole deep muffin tray, well greased or lined
    with paper muffin cases (see note)

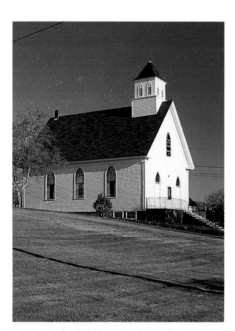

In New England, white-painted churches like this
are a familiar sight. The one shown above is at
Mackerel Bay, Maine.

To me, muffins mean New England, and the best ones are made with the tart juicy fruit of that region – cranberries and wild blueberries, either fresh or frozen. This is my mother-in-law's recipe. The combination of white and stoneground wholemeal flour gives a good texture and prevents these muffins tasting like fairy cakes; the orange contrasts well with the mouth-puckering tartness of the cranberries. Eat warm, preferably on the day of baking.

Preheat the oven to 200C (400F, Gas 6).

Mix the flours with the baking powder, salt, sugar and grated orange rind in a mixing bowl. Mix the egg, milk, orange juice and oil together, then add to the dry ingredients and mix with a wooden spoon until almost evenly blended. Add the fruit and briefly mix again – too much mixing can make the muffins tough.

Spoon the mixture into the prepared tray, dividing equally among the holes. Bake for 20–25 minutes or until a cocktail stick inserted into the centre of a muffin comes out clean. The muffins should be golden and firm, with a distinct cracked peak. Leave the muffins to cool in the tray for a minute, then turn out on to a wire rack to cool for a further few minutes. Eat while still warm, with or without butter.

VARIATION: BLUEBERRY MUFFINS Replace the cranberries with an equal quantity of fresh or frozen blueberries. Omit the orange rind, and replace the orange juice with an equal quantity of lemon juice. You could also use blackberries, raspberries or stoned cherries.

NOTE Be sure to use deep muffin trays; traditional English bun tins are too shallow. The individual hole, or cup, should be about 6.5cm (2⅝in) deep. For stockists, see page 190.

BURN O'VAT ROCK CAKES

INGREDIENTS

Makes about 8

230g (8oz) self-raising flour

¼ teaspoon ground mixed spice

85g (3oz) unsalted butter, chilled and diced

85g (3oz) golden granulated sugar

110g (4oz) mixed dried fruit and chopped candied
   peel

1 egg

2 tablespoons milk

1 tablespoon demerara sugar for sprinkling

2 baking trays, greased

I'm very fond of good rock cakes, which should be moist, crumbly, slightly spicy and with a fair amount of dried fruit and candied peel. I got this recipe 20 years ago from a tiny tea shop, now closed, at Burn O'Vat — a beauty spot near Ballater in Aberdeenshire. I always bake a batch for picnics on long car and boat trips.

Preheat the oven to 200C (400F, Gas 6).

Sift the flour and spice into a mixing bowl. Add the diced butter and rub it into the flour with your fingertips until the mixture resembles fine crumbs. Stir in the sugar and the dried fruit and peel. Mix the egg with the milk, and stir just enough into the fruit mixture to bind to a firm, stiff dough — it is important that the dough holds its shape.

Divide the dough into eight portions and spoon on to the prepared baking trays in heaped, peaky mounds spaced well apart. Sprinkle with the demerara sugar. Bake for 12–15 minutes or until golden brown. Transfer to a wire rack to cool completely. Eat the same day or the following day, warmed and spread with butter.

COOL THE ROCK CAKES ON A WIRE RACK.

RIGHT For many years, visitors to the Highlands, including Queen Victoria, used to take the steam train from Aberdeen to Ballater.

CAROLL'S BROWNIES

INGREDIENTS

Makes 16 squares
140g (5oz) unsalted butter
4 eggs
340g (12oz) caster sugar
1 teaspoon pure vanilla essence
¼ teaspoon salt
80g (2¾oz) cocoa powder
140g (5oz) plain flour
110g (4oz) walnut pieces

a 23cm (9in) square tin, about 5cm (2in) deep,
   completely lined with greased foil

After intensive research, Anthony and I have decided that this is the best recipe for brownies we have ever eaten. It is also one of the simplest. It comes from a good friend and good cook, Caroll Boltin, a food historian who lives in the Hudson Valley in New York state.

Making a good brownie — one that is moist and fudgy rather than dry and spongy — requires great self-restraint. The melted butter must be cool when it is added or it will cook the eggs. If you beat the eggs and sugar too vigorously, too much air will be incorporated and the brownies will be more like a cake. The final mixture should be gently stirred rather than beaten, or the brownies will be tough and dry. Most important of all, it is vital to avoid overcooking — Caroll's tip is to test by inserting a skewer halfway between the centre and the side of the tin — the centre should remain quite moist. It is also a good idea to wrap the cooled cake and keep it overnight before cutting into squares — if you can wait.

Preheat the oven to 170C (325F, Gas 3).

Very gently melt the butter and leave to cool. Using a wooden spoon gently beat the eggs with the sugar until well blended and creamy looking. Stir in the cooled butter and the vanilla. Sift the salt, cocoa and flour together and add to the mixture. Stir until thoroughly blended, then fold in the nuts. Pour the mixture into the prepared tin. Bake for about 40 minutes or until a skewer inserted midway between the centre and the side of the tin comes out clean.

Cool in the tin for a few minutes, then lift the cake, still in the foil, out of the tin on to a wire rack. When completely cold, remove the foil and cut into 16 squares. Very good with vanilla ice-cream.

VARIATIONS For children who can't eat nuts I make the same mixture, substituting 110g (4oz) best quality white chocolate, coarsely chopped, for the walnuts. For parties I double the recipe and bake it in a roasting tin lined with foil.

The best brownies ever — moist and fudgy, with lots of walnuts.

BROWN SUGAR MERINGUES

INGREDIENTS

Makes 4 pairs
2 egg whites
a pinch of cream of tartar (optional)
110g (4oz) light muscovado sugar, sifted

FILLING:
140ml (5fl oz) double or whipping cream, chilled
45g (1½oz) stem ginger, drained of syrup, finely
   chopped

2 baking trays, lined with non-stick baking
   parchment or re-usable silicon lining

1 WHISK THE SUGAR INTO THE EGG WHITES
TO MAKE A GLOSSY, FIRM MERINGUE.

2 USE A COUPLE OF SERVING SPOONS TO
HEAP THE MERINGUE ON BAKING TRAYS.

The rich caramel flavour of these meringues comes from light muscovado raw cane sugar. Although the meringue mixture is made in the usual way, it is important to sift the sugar so that pockets of melted sugar do not form during baking. Use egg whites that are several days old — or add a pinch of cream of tartar if they are very fresh — and have them at room temperature. Pairs of meringues can be sandwiched together with ginger cream, as here, or you can use the chocolate filling for the macaroons on page 24.

Preheat the oven to 130C (250F, Gas ½).

Put the egg whites and cream of tartar into a spotlessly clean, grease-free bowl (avoid plastic if possible as it is difficult to keep really clean). Whisk, slowly at first and then gradually increasing the speed, until the whites form a smooth foam that will stand in soft peaks. Take care not to overwhisk the meringue to stiff peaks or it will collapse during baking. Whisk in the sugar a tablespoon at a time. The final meringue should form firm peaks when the whisk is lifted out.

Spoon on to the prepared baking trays to form 8 even-sized heaps. Bake in the preheated oven for 3–4 hours or until firm, dry and crisp. Leave to cool completely, then store in an airtight tin until ready to assemble — they can be kept for a week at this stage.

To finish, whip the cream until stiff and stir in the ginger. Use to sandwich pairs of meringues together. Eat immediately if you like crisp meringues — after a couple of hours they become slightly and deliciously gooey, which is how I like them.

CHAPTER TWO

PUDDINGS & DESSERTS

Although taken to be synonymous, there
is a difference between a pudding and a dessert.
Traditionally, puddings are made with flour, eggs
and milk or cream, while desserts are based
on fruit. The word dessert comes from the
French desservir, meaning to clear the
table of plates and sweep the crumbs
from the cloth ready for the last,
most decorative course.

QUEEN OF PUDDINGS

Serves 4

85g (3oz) fresh white breadcrumbs or spongecake crumbs

100g (3¹/₂oz) caster sugar

the grated rind of 1 large unwaxed lemon

430ml (15fl oz) creamy milk

45g (1¹/₂oz) unsalted butter

3 eggs, size 2, separated

4 tablespoons strawberry conserve, preferably Little Scarlet

4 ramekins of 300ml (10¹/₂fl oz) capacity, greased

The best English puddings are the old-fashioned nursery favourites. I am not sure where this recipe comes from, but along with chocolate Castle Puddings (see opposite), it was one of my childhood treats. You can use any good jam or conserve, or even lemon curd (see page 129).

Preheat the oven to 170C (325F, Gas 3).

Put the crumbs and 1 tablespoon of the sugar into a mixing bowl and stir in the lemon rind. Heat the milk with the butter in a saucepan until the butter just melts, then pour the mixture over the crumbs and stir well. Leave to soak for 15 minutes. Stir in the egg yolks.

Divide the custard mixture among the prepared ramekins and bake in the preheated oven for 15–20 minutes or until the custards are just set and firm to the touch. Remove from the oven and spoon the jam on to the surface of the custards.

Whisk the egg whites in a spotlessly clean, grease-free bowl until they form stiff peaks. Gradually whisk in the remaining sugar to make a stiff glossy meringue. Spoon the meringue on top of the jam. Return the ramekins to the oven and bake for about 10 minutes or until the meringue topping is lightly browned.

Serve warm or at room temperature, with cream or fromage frais.

BAKE QUEEN OF PUDDINGS JUST UNTIL THE MERINGUE TOPPING IS LIGHTLY BROWNED.

PREVIOUS PAGE At the end of an afternoon of baking, Dee Dee Meyer finishes icing a raspberry torte.

CASTLE PUDDINGS

INGREDIENTS

Makes 8
SPONGE PUDDINGS:
110g (4oz) unsalted butter, at room temperature
110g (4oz) golden caster sugar
2 eggs, beaten
85g (3oz) self-raising flour
½ teaspoon baking powder
30g (1oz) ground almonds
15g (½oz) cocoa powder
1 tablespoon milk

SAUCE:
430ml (15fl oz) creamy milk
20g (¾oz) cocoa powder
60g (2oz) caster sugar
15g (½oz) cornflour
2 egg yolks

8 dariole moulds of about 85ml (3fl oz) capacity,
    greased

These are chocolate and almond sponge puddings, baked in dariole moulds, then turned out and served with chocolate custard. When I was small, I pretended they were Saracen castles surrounded by moats; like any good Crusader I demolished them completely.

Preheat the oven to 180C (350F, Gas 4).

To make the puddings, beat the butter until creamy, using a wooden spoon or electric mixer. Gradually beat in the sugar. When the mixture is very light and fluffy, beat in the eggs a tablespoon at a time, beating well after each addition. Sift the flour with the baking powder, ground almonds and cocoa powder, then fold into the beaten mixture with the milk, using a large metal spoon.

Spoon the mixture into the prepared moulds, which should be two-thirds full. Stand the moulds in a bain-marie – a roasting tin half-filled with very hot water. Cover the whole thing with foil, then bake in the preheated oven for about 30 minutes or until firm.

Meanwhile, make the sauce. Heat the milk in a heavy saucepan until scalding hot. Sift the cocoa, sugar and cornflour into a mixing bowl. Stir in the egg yolks to make a smooth, thick paste, then stir in the hot milk. When thoroughly blended, pour the mixture into the saucepan and stir over low heat until thickened – do not let the sauce boil.

To serve, carefully loosen the puddings with a small palette knife or round-bladed knife, and turn out on to a deep dish or individual plates. Spoon the sauce around the base of the puddings and eat immediately. Allow two puddings per adult, one for a child.

LITTLE CHRISTMAS PUDDINGS

INGREDIENTS

Makes about 12

60g (2oz) unsalted butter, at room temperature

60g (2oz) honey

2 eggs, beaten

110g (4oz) ready-to-eat dried figs, chopped

110g (4oz) blanched almonds, chopped

60g (2oz) pine nuts

60g (2oz) currants

110g (4oz) raisins

60g (2oz) sultanas

1 small apple, such as a Cox's Orange Pippin,
    peeled, cored and grated

1/2 teaspoon ground mixed spice

60g (2oz) dark muscovado sugar

110g (4oz) fresh white breadcrumbs

60g (2oz) mixed candied peel, finely chopped

a pinch of salt

the grated rind and juice of 1 small, or 1/2 large,
    unwaxed lemon

12 dariole moulds of about 85ml (3fl oz) capacity,
    greased

As I discovered, by accident, these individual Christmas puddings can be baked rather than steamed, as is traditional. The recipe is wonderfully odd: it contains no flour, just breadcrumbs, and has no suet, just butter. It also contains plenty of nuts, almonds and pine nuts, honey as well as dark muscovado sugar, and figs along with the other dried fruits. It is so good I no longer make the traditional sticky-rich pudding. Once the ingredients are assembled, the pudding is quick and simple enough to make for a winter Sunday lunch. Serve with brandy butter, cream or ice-cream.

Preheat the oven to 170C (325F, Gas 3).

Put the butter into a large mixing bowl and beat until creamy, using a wooden spoon or electric mixer. Beat in the honey. Gradually beat in the eggs, a tablespoon at a time. The mixture will resemble scrambled eggs at this point. Put all the other ingredients into another bowl and mix well. Stir into the butter mixture. When thoroughly blended, spoon into the prepared dariole moulds – they should be seven-eighths full. Cover each mould with a piece of greased greaseproof paper, pleated in the middle, then tie it on with string.

Set the moulds in a bain-marie – a roasting tin half-filled with very hot water. Cover the whole thing with foil and bake in the preheated oven for about 1 hour or until the puddings are firm to the touch and have shrunk slightly from the sides of the moulds.

Carefully loosen the puddings using a small palette knife, then turn out on to individual serving plates and serve hot.

LEFT Serve Little Christmas Puddings hot, dusted with icing sugar.

BEAT THE EGGS WITH A FORK UNTIL WELL MIXED, THEN BEAT INTO THE HONEY MIXTURE.

DOTTY'S BAKED OATMEAL

Serves 6
115ml (4fl oz) soya or sunflower oil
2 eggs, beaten
170g (6oz) caster sugar
280g (10oz) porridge oats
2 teaspoons baking powder
$^1/_2$ teaspoon salt
230ml (8fl oz) whole milk

TO SERVE:
chopped fresh peaches or strawberries
single cream

a deep baking dish or soufflé dish, about 20.5cm
   (8in) in diameter, greased

RIGHT Dottie and Andy Hess serve their guests a hearty farmhouse breakfast, which usually includes Baked Oatmeal with a fresh fruit compote.

Dotty and Andy Hess have a 170-acre family farm, mainly cattle, pigs and corn, at Mount Joy in Lancaster County, Pennsylvania. Since their seven children have now left home, Dotty has converted the bedrooms of their pretty farmhouse to take in bed and breakfast guests.

Staying with the Hess family was a real treat for us: the rooms are charmingly decorated and exquisitely comfortable, with a candle light in each window in the local Mennonite style. The highlight of each day was a hearty farmhouse breakfast made almost entirely with home-grown ingredients. One morning Dotty greeted us with glee — she had just cut the first asparagus spears of the season and was about to cook them with the breakfast eggs.

To whet our appetite — as if she needed to — she gave us baked oatmeal. It is nothing like porridge, but rather resembles an oatmeal muffin. It was accompanied by a compote of peaches that had grown in the back garden. The dish was so good that Dotty made it for us again the next morning, this time with her strawberries. This is her recipe, which I like to make for family lunches — it has become a favourite.

Preheat the oven to 180C (350F, Gas 4).
   Mix the oil with the eggs and sugar. When thoroughly blended, stir in the oats, baking powder and salt followed by the milk. Mix well, then pour into the prepared baking dish.
   Bake for 35–40 minutes or until golden and firm to the touch. Serve warm, with the fresh fruit and cream.

VARIATION Dotty sometimes adds grated raw apples, ground cinnamon and chopped walnuts or pecans to the mixture before pouring it into the baking dish.

CHERRY CLAFOUTIS

INGREDIENTS

Makes a 20.5cm (8in) flan, to serve 4–6

PASTRY:

170g (6oz) self-raising flour

a pinch of salt

2 tablespoons caster sugar

85g (3oz) unsalted butter, chilled and diced

1 egg yolk, mixed with 2 tablespoons icy water

FILLING:

450g (1lb) ripe cherries, stoned, or a 411g
  (14½oz) can stoned black cherries, drained

85ml (3fl oz) single or double cream

2 eggs, size 2, beaten

3 tablespoons ground almonds

1 tablespoon kirsch or brandy

20g (¾oz) unsalted butter, melted

a 20.5cm (8in) loose-based flan tin

a baking tray

The classic French clafoutis is a cross between an egg custard and a Yorkshire pudding studded with fruit. This is a version of chef Roger Vergé's very rich, very light clafoutis with a pastry base. Fresh cherries work best, but frozen or canned cherries are good too, as are fresh or ready-to-eat dried apricots, or ready-to-eat prunes.

To make the pastry, put the flour, salt and sugar into the bowl of a food processor and briefly mix. Add the diced butter and process until the mixture resembles fine crumbs. With the machine running, add the yolk mixture through the feed tube. As soon as the dough comes together, stop the machine – the dough should be soft but not sticky. Alternatively, the dough can be made by hand (see page 132). Wrap and chill for 10 minutes.

Preheat the oven to 200C (400F, Gas 6). Put a baking tray in the oven to heat up.

Roll out the pastry dough on a lightly floured work surface to a round about 25.5cm (10in) in diameter. Using the rolling pin as a support lift the dough and drape it over the flan tin. Gently press the dough into the tin to line the sides and bottom. Trim off any excess dough, and prick the bottom all over with a fork. Chill for 10 minutes.

Line the pastry case with a piece of greaseproof paper and fill with baking beans. Set the flan tin on the preheated baking tray and bake the pastry case blind for 10 minutes. Carefully remove the paper and beans – the pastry will still be soft. Return the flan case to the oven and bake for a further 5 minutes or until firm and lightly golden. Remove the tin from the oven, leaving the baking tray inside. Do not turn out the flan case.

Make sure the cherries are thoroughly drained. Put the cream, eggs, ground almonds and kirsch or brandy in a bowl and mix thoroughly, then mix in the melted butter. Arrange the cherries in the flan case, then gently pour over the custard mixture. Set the flan tin on the hot baking tray again and bake for 15–20 minutes or until the filling is golden and set. Carefully remove the clafoutis from the tin and serve warm, with cream.

Above CAREFULLY POUR THE RICH EGG CUSTARD MIXTURE OVER THE FRUIT IN THE BAKED PASTRY CASE.

DEE DEE'S RASPBERRY TORTE

INGREDIENTS

Serves 8

BASE:

200g (7oz) plain flour

1 teaspoon baking powder

60g (2oz) caster sugar

110g (4oz) butter, at room temperature

1 egg, beaten

85g (3oz) raspberry jam

FILLING:

110g (4oz) caster sugar

110g (4oz) butter, at room temperature

$^{1}/_{2}$ teaspoon pure almond essence

2 eggs, beaten

2–3 tablespoons flaked almonds for sprinkling

TOPPING:

85g (3oz) raspberry jam

60g (2oz) icing sugar, sifted

about 2 teaspoons lemon juice

a 25.5–28cm (10–11in) springclip tin, greased

BELOW Dee Dee's children — even the youngest —
help her prepare dinner for her guests.

While staying with Dotty and Andy Hess we were invited to dine with a family who belong to the Old Order River Brethren. Dee Dee and Jack Meyer and their six children live near Manheim, in a house built with the help of their Amish friends. The Old Order communities — the Amish, the Mennonites and the Brethren — came to Pennsylvania from the German part of Switzerland in the early 18th century. Jack explained that all stemmed from the Anabaptists — rebaptisers — who believe in making a conscious choice to accept God and only baptise adults.

So-called 'Pennsylvania Dutch' cooking has a strong German influence. It is an oral tradition, taught from one generation to the next, and each nutritious meal is prepared from scratch. The dishes are hearty and simple — most farming families eat three full meals a day. The ingredients are those easily obtainable from local farms: beef, chicken and pork; potatoes, sweetcorn and cucumbers; milk and eggs; grains and beans; apples and soft fruits. Fruit and vegetables are preserved by canning, bottling and pickling.

Dinner at the Meyers was memorable. Dee Dee and a friend spent most of the afternoon cooking for the eight members of the family and fourteen guests. As the children arrived home from school, even the smallest were given tasks. We all dined at one long table, lit by oil lamps, and Jack explained that they enjoyed the opportunity to entertain paying guests: 'It is good for other people to see how we live, to share a meal with us, to ask questions.' To go hungry is to ignore the bounty of the earth, and the Old Order Communities take advantage of every occasion — weddings, barn raisings, Sabbath dinners — to enjoy a delicious meal together.

To make the base, put the flour, baking powder and sugar into a mixing bowl, and stir to combine. Add the butter and egg and work the ingredients together, using a round-bladed knife, a fork or wooden spoon, until the mixture resembles coarse crumbs. Using your hands, press the crumbs together, then gently knead to make a shortbread-like dough.

With the heel of your hand, press the dough into the bottom of the prepared tin to make an even layer. Spread the jam over the base, then chill for 10 minutes. Meanwhile, preheat the oven to 180C (350F, Gas 4).

To make the filling, put the sugar, butter, almond essence and eggs into a mixing bowl. Using an electric mixer, beat until very light and fluffy.

Spoon the mixture on to the jam-covered base and spread evenly. Sprinkle with the flaked almonds.

Bake for about 40 minutes or until firm and golden. Leave to cool until the torte is firm enough to handle, then unclip the side of the tin and carefully remove it.

Beat the jam to soften it a little, then gently spread over the top of the torte. Mix the icing sugar with enough lemon juice to make a smooth and pourable icing. Using a small spoon, drizzle the icing over the torte. Serve warm or at room temperature, within 24 hours of baking.

ABOVE The farmhouse the Meyers built at Manheim, Pennsylvania.

RIGHT Dee Dee Meyer.

BREAD AND BUTTER PUDDING

INGREDIENTS

Serves 4–6
280ml (10fl oz) creamy milk
280ml (10fl oz) single cream
1 vanilla pod, split
a pinch of salt
4 eggs
110g (4oz) caster sugar or vanilla sugar
5 thin slices, about 170g (6oz), tea bread
   (page 96), white bread or brioche (page 90)
about 45g (1½oz) unsalted butter, at room
   temperature
icing sugar for sprinkling

a shallow baking dish of about 1.15 litres (2 pints)
   capacity, buttered

The basic recipe for this old-fashioned but now highly fashionable pudding uses four eggs to one pint of liquid for the custard and some bread. The liquid can be milk, cream or a combination. The bread can be plain white, brioche, croissant or, as here, a fruited tea bread. The bread is usually spread with butter, but I have eaten very good puddings where the bread has been spread with marmalade or lemon curd.

Put the milk, cream, vanilla pod and salt into a saucepan and heat slowly until scalding hot. Remove from the heat, cover and set aside to infuse for 20 minutes.

Put the eggs and sugar into a large wide-mouthed jug or mixing bowl and lightly whisk together. Remove the vanilla pod from the milk mixture, then whisk into the egg mixture.

Butter the bread. Cut each slice in half diagonally, and cut off the crusts if you like. Arrange in the prepared baking dish so the top edges of each piece of bread are above the rim. Carefully pour the custard down the sides of the dish. Leave to stand for 2 hours.

When ready to cook preheat the oven to 170C (325F, Gas 3). Stand the baking dish in a bain-marie – a roasting tin half-filled with lukewarm water – and bake for about 40 minutes or until just firm to the touch. If the custard is overcooked, it will separate and become watery.

Heat the grill. Remove the baking dish from the bain-marie and sprinkle the top of the pudding with sifted icing sugar. Put the dish under the hot grill for a few seconds, until the sugar is golden and caramelised. Serve warm or at room temperature, with cream or ice-cream.

Above AS YOU POUR THE CUSTARD INTO THE DISH, CAREFULLY LIFT THE BREAD SO THE CUSTARD CAN MOISTEN ALL THE SLICES.

Right THE PUDDING IS COOKED WHEN IT IS JUST FIRM TO THE TOUCH IN THE CENTRE.

CHOCOLATE BREAD PUDDING

INGREDIENTS

Serves 4–6

170g (6oz) plain or chocolate brioche (page 90),
    challah or milk bread

710ml (1¼ pints) creamy milk

50g (1¾oz) caster sugar

3 eggs, size 2, beaten

110g (4oz) raisins

40g (1½oz) toasted hazelnuts, finely chopped

a few drops of pure vanilla essence

100g (3½oz) good dark chocolate, finely grated or
    melted

2 teaspoons baking powder

1 teaspoon ground cinnamon

¼ teaspoon freshly grated nutmeg

60g (2oz) unsalted butter

a baking dish of about 1.15 litres (2 pints)
    capacity, buttered

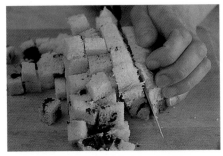

Above USE A LARGE KNIFE TO CUT THE BRIOCHE INTO NEAT, SMALL DICE.

Above right TO ENSURE THAT THE PUDDING IS MOIST, TAKE IT OUT OF THE OVEN AS SOON AS IT IS DONE.

Kenny's restaurant serves the best Cajun and Creole food in London. It is owned and run by a Scot who's proud to be an honorary citizen of New Orleans — as a mere non-resident alien spouse of an American, I'm jealous. Kenny's puddings are served in magnificently large portions, and this is my favourite. He serves it with ice-cream or egg custard flavoured with bourbon.

Dice the brioche, challah or bread, discarding the crusts. Mix the milk with the sugar and eggs in a mixing bowl. Stir in the cubes of bread and leave to soak for 30 minutes.

Meanwhile, preheat the oven to 170C (325F, Gas 3).

Stir the raisins, hazelnuts, vanilla and chocolate into the bread mixture. Sift the baking powder with the spices and stir in. Spoon or pour into the prepared baking dish and dot the top with the butter.

Bake for 1–1¼ hours or until just firm to the touch. Serve hot or warm, on its own or with ice-cream or custard.

TURKISH LEMON PUDDING

INGREDIENTS

Serves 6–8

300g (10¹/₂oz) plain flour

340g (12oz) golden caster sugar

3 eggs, size 2

230ml (8fl oz) plain yogurt, preferably thick
   Turkish or Greek yogurt

1¹/₂ teaspoons bicarbonate of soda

the juice of ¹/₂ lemon

115ml (4fl oz) boiling water

clotted cream to serve

SYRUP:

455ml (16fl oz) water

450g (1lb) golden caster sugar

the juice of 1¹/₂ lemons

a baking dish, about 20.5 x 30.5cm (8 x 12in),
   greased

This recipe comes from my friend, Zeynep Conker Stromfelt, whose mother is pastry chef at a top Istanbul restaurant. Zeynep is a living cookbook of classic Turkish recipes, but she is especially fond of this typical family pudding: 'It comes from my grandmother; it is quick and simple to prepare, and my children adore it.' The unusual batter bakes to a very light sponge which is then soaked, like a baba, in a sweet, very lemony syrup. I thought it would be made with honey, but Zeynep explained that honey is not used in Turkish cooking.

Preheat the oven to 170C (325F, Gas 3).

Put the flour into a mixing bowl and stir in the sugar, then the eggs. Add the yogurt, bicarbonate of soda and lemon juice. Mix thoroughly to make a very thick, lump-free batter. Pour into the prepared baking dish and bake for 45 minutes to 1 hour or until a skewer inserted into the centre comes out clean. The sponge will peak in the centre.

While the sponge is baking, make the syrup. Boil the water in a medium-sized saucepan, then add the sugar and stir over low heat until dissolved. Bring back to the boil and boil for 1 minute, then remove from the heat and add the lemon juice. For an even more intense flavour you can add grated lemon rind to taste, but this is less popular with children. Keep the syrup hot.

As soon as the sponge comes out of the oven, loosen the edges and prick it all over with a skewer. Pour over the boiling water. Cover with foil and leave to stand for about 10 minutes or until the water has been completely absorbed.

Prick the sponge again, then slowly spoon over the very hot syrup – it will gradually be absorbed and the sponge will swell. Serve at room temperature, with clotted cream.

This pudding is best when quickly made and immediately baked, so Zeynep assembles all the ingredients before she starts work. The sponge is unusual in that it contains yogurt.

MOTHER-IN-LAW'S APPLE CRISP

INGREDIENTS

Serves 4–6

6 large tart apples, such as Granny Smiths,
   Bramleys
230g (8oz) blueberries – fresh or use from frozen
the grated rind and juice of 1 small unwaxed lemon
sugar (optional)

TOPPING:
140g (5oz) plain flour
100g (3½oz) light muscovado sugar
110g (4oz) unsalted butter, diced
170–230g (6–8oz) walnut pieces

a large shallow baking dish, lightly greased

When we visit my husband's family at Yarmouth, Maine, everyone gathers together for our first dinner at home. Each member of the family cooks something, and dessert is always the same – my mother-in-law's apple and blueberry crisp. Annette got this recipe from her mother-in-law, so by giving it to me she establishes a family tradition. I prefer this fruit crisp to its English cousin, the apple crumble, because the topping is lighter and crunchier. As with a crumble, you can vary the fruit filling to suit the season – peach and raspberry, blackberry and apple or pear, pear and prune, plum and orange, apricot and banana, rhubarb and redcurrant. The blueberries that grow wild up on the Maine coast are a delicacy – small but very juicy with a distinct tartness, which is enhanced by a little lemon rind and juice.

Preheat the oven to 190C (375F, Gas 5).

Peel, core and dice the apples. Put into a bowl with the blueberries and the grated lemon rind and juice. Toss gently until thoroughly mixed. Add a little sugar (light muscovado or caster) to taste if using sour or very tart fruit – eating apples usually don't need sugar. Put the fruit into the prepared baking dish in an even layer.

To make the topping, combine the flour and sugar in a mixing bowl. Add the butter and rub and squeeze into the flour mixture – it should not look like breadcrumbs but rather form flakes or pea-sized lumps of dough. Stir in the nuts. Sprinkle the topping evenly over the fruit.

Bake for about 30 minutes or until the fruit is tender but not mushy, and the topping is crisp and golden. The fruit juices will probably bubble up through the topping in places giving a crazy-paving look. Eat warm or at room temperature, within 24 hours, with ice-cream, yogurt, fromage frais or cream.

ABOVE *Yarmouth, Maine, where my husband's family live.*

OPPOSITE *My mother-in-law Annette lends me her kitchen as well as her best recipes.*

FRUIT BASKETS

INGREDIENTS

Serves 6
BISCUITS:
1 egg white, size 2
60g (2oz) caster sugar
30g (1oz) unsalted butter, melted and cooled
30g (1oz) plain flour, sifted
the grated rind of ¹/₂ unwaxed orange
60g (2oz) good dark chocolate, chopped

CREME ANGLAISE:
140ml (5fl oz) very creamy milk or single cream
3 egg yolks, size 2
30g (1oz) caster sugar, or to taste
the grated rind of ¹/₂ unwaxed orange
1 tablespoon orange liqueur

FRUIT FILLING:
about 340g (12oz) prepared fresh fruit, such as a
    mixture of raspberries, strawberries, grapes,
    apples, currants, mango, plum, peach — whatever
    is available
3 tablespoons orange juice or orange liqueur

several baking trays, greased
small individual brioche moulds, squat tumblers or
    oranges, lightly greased

These delicate crisp biscuit baskets are made with a basic tuile mixture. They are dipped in chocolate, just to coat the rim, and are filled with fresh fruit salad and served with crème anglaise. The baskets are shaped by draping the just-cooked biscuits over an oiled brioche mould, though a small tumbler or cup, or even an orange, could be substituted. The recipe will make more biscuits than you need, to allow for failures or breakages.

Preheat the oven to 180C (350F, Gas 4).

To make the biscuit baskets, put the egg white into a spotlessly clean, grease-free, non-plastic bowl. Whisk until stiff, then gradually whisk in the sugar, followed by the cooled melted butter and, finally, the sifted flour. If using an electric mixer, do this on low speed. Gently stir in the grated orange rind.

Spoon a teaspoon of the mixture on to a prepared baking tray and spread into a thin disc about 10cm (4in) in diameter. Bake for about 5 minutes or until a pale gold colour. Remove from the oven. Using a palette knife, immediately loosen the biscuit from the baking tray and quickly

drape it over a mould or orange – it will harden very rapidly. Leave to cool before removing from the mould or orange. Once you have got the knack of this process you can bake the biscuits two at a time.

To finish the baskets, melt the chocolate on a heatproof plate set over a pan of hot but not boiling water. Turn each basket upside down and dip the rim into the melted chocolate. Turn the right way up and leave to set. You will need 6 baskets.

To make the crème anglaise, heat the milk in a heavy saucepan until scalding hot. Cream the egg yolks with the sugar until thick and pale, then gradually stir in the hot milk. Stir thoroughly, then pour into the rinsed out milk pan. Cook over very low heat, stirring constantly with a wooden spoon, until the custard thickens enough to coat the back of the spoon. This can take as much as 5 minutes. Do not be tempted to hurry the process; if the custard boils it will curdle and cannot be used. Strain the thickened custard into a jug and stir in the orange rind and liqueur. Sprinkle the surface of the custard with a little sugar to prevent a skin forming. Leave to cool, then cover and chill.

When ready to serve, set a basket on each dessert plate. Toss the prepared fruit with the juice or liqueur, then spoon into the baskets. Spoon a little crème anglaise around the base of each basket. Eat immediately.

RICH CHOCOLATE SOUFFLÉ

This exceedingly rich, classic French soufflé is like a hot chocolate mousse. It is made without flour, and has a light, meltingly soft texture. For the best taste you should use the finest dark chocolate you can find – with at least 70% cocoa solids. Most supermarkets now stock this. The method is quick and straightforward – if you can make meringue you can make this soufflé.

Preheat the oven to 220C (425F, Gas 7).

Brush the ramekins with melted butter, then sprinkle with caster sugar to make an even coating on the bottom and sides. This will help the soufflé mixture to rise well and evenly, as well as giving a nice crunchy thin crust. Stand the prepared ramekins on a baking sheet or in a roasting tin.

Put the chocolate into a heavy-based pan with the cream. Set over very low heat and stir occasionally until melted. Remove from the heat and stir until smooth. Gently stir in the egg yolks, one at a time, and then the brandy. Set aside.

Put the 5 egg whites into a spotlessly clean, grease-free bowl and whisk until stiff peaks form. Sprinkle with the sugar and briefly whisk again to make a smooth, stiff meringue. If you overwhisk the meringue at this stage (it will start to look grainy), it will do more harm than good, and the end result will be less smooth.

The chocolate mixture should be just warm, so gently reheat it if necessary. Using a large metal spoon add a little of the meringue to the chocolate mixture and mix until thoroughly combined. This 'softens' the chocolate – loosens the consistency – to make it easier to combine with the meringue. Pour the chocolate mixture on top of the remaining meringue in the bowl and gently fold the two mixtures together until thoroughly combined but not over-mixed.

Spoon or pour into the prepared ramekins: the soufflé mixture should come to just below the rim. Bake at once, for 8–10 minutes. Remove from the oven when they are barely set: the centres should be soft and wobble when gently shaken. Sprinkle with sifted icing sugar and eat immediately.

1 COMBINE THE DOUBLE CREAM AND PIECES OF CHOCOLATE IN A SAUCEPAN.

2 HEAT GENTLY UNTIL MELTED. REMOVE FROM THE HEAT AND STIR UNTIL SMOOTH.

3 ADD THE EGG YOLKS TO THE CHOCOLATE MIXTURE, ONE AT A TIME, STIRRING.

4 ADD THE BRANDY AND STIR UNTIL IT HAS BEEN COMPLETELY BLENDED IN.

5 THE CHOCOLATE MIXTURE SHOULD BE VERY SMOOTH AND GLOSSY. SET IT ASIDE.

6 WHISK THE EGG WHITES UNTIL STIFF, THEN ADD THE SUGAR AND WHISK BRIEFLY.

7 ADD A SPOONFUL OF THE MERINGUE TO THE WARM CHOCOLATE MIXTURE.

8 POUR THE CHOCOLATE MIXTURE ON TO THE REMAINING MERINGUE IN THE BOWL.

9 GENTLY FOLD THE TWO MIXTURES TOGETHER UNTIL EVENLY COMBINED.

10 DIVIDE THE SOUFFLÉ MIXTURE AMONG THE RAMEKIN DISHES AND BAKE AT ONCE.

ALMOND AND APPLE SLICE

In this Swiss recipe, rich, crisp sweet pastry is covered with fried almonds, topped with a mound of apples and finished with a marzipan lattice. It is substantial but not too rich, and can be made several hours before serving.

To make the pastry, put the flour, salt and sugar into the bowl of a food processor and mix briefly. Add the butter and process until the mixture resembles coarse crumbs. With the machine running, add the egg yolks through the feed tube, and process until the mixture forms large clumps. Do not overprocess or the dough will be greasy and heavy. Turn the dough on to the work surface and gather into a ball. Wrap and chill until firm – about 45 minutes. Meanwhile, heat the oven to 190C (375F, Gas 5).

Roll out the pastry dough on a lightly floured work surface to an 11.5 x 30.5cm (4½ x 12in) rectangle that is about 6mm (¼in) thick. Roll the rectangle around the rolling pin and transfer it to the prepared baking tray. If necessary neaten the edges either by trimming with a large sharp knife or by gently shaping with your hands. Flute the edges with your fingers, and prick the pastry rectangle well all over with a fork. Chill for about 15 minutes or until firm.

Bake for 10–12 minutes or until golden and firm. Cool for a minute, then loosen the underside with a large spatula. Leave to cool on the baking tray. Increase the oven temperature to 220C (425F, Gas 7).

While the pastry base is cooling, make the filling. Mix the sultanas with the rum and set aside to soak. Peel, core and thickly slice the apples. Mix with the sultanas and any soaking liquid left. Add the cinnamon. Toss well, then tip into a baking dish or roasting tin. Bake for 15 minutes or until the apples are barely tender. Leave to cool in the dish.

Melt the butter in a small heavy pan. Add the chopped almonds and mixed spice and cook gently, stirring frequently, for 5 minutes or until golden. Leave to cool.

INGREDIENTS

Cuts into 8 slices
PASTRY:
110g (4oz) plain flour
a pinch of salt
60g (2oz) golden caster sugar
60g (2oz) unsalted butter, chilled and diced
2 egg yolks

FILLING:
60g (2oz) sultanas
3 tablespoons rum or fruit juice
680g (1½lb) dessert apples – Cox's Orange
    Pippins for choice
1 teaspoon ground cinnamon
30g (1oz) unsalted butter
60g (2oz) blanched almonds, roughly chopped
1 teaspoon ground mixed spice

TOPPING:
1 egg white
1 tablespoon plain flour
340g (12oz) white marzipan

TO FINISH:
2–3 tablespoons sieved apricot jam, warmed, for
    glazing
about 30g (1oz) toasted flaked almonds for
    sprinkling

a baking tray, greased
a piping bag fitted with a 1cm (³⁄₈in) plain tube

DECORATE THE EDGE OF THE PASTRY RECTANGLE BY FLUTING WITH YOUR FINGERS.

OPEN OUT THE PIPING BAG AND STAND IT UPRIGHT IN A JUG FOR SUPPORT, THEN SPOON IN THE MARZIPAN MIXTURE.

PIPE THE MARZIPAN MIXTURE OVER THE APPLE TOPPING TO MAKE A ZIG-ZAG LATTICE PATTERN.

To make the topping, put the egg white and flour in a food processor. Break up the marzipan with your hands and add to the processor. Process until smooth. If it is a very hot day and the mixture seems too difficult and runny to pipe, put it in the fridge to chill for 30 minutes. Spoon the mixture into the piping bag fitted with the plain tube.

To finish the slice, preheat the oven to 230C (450F, Gas 8). Spoon the nut mixture on to the pastry base on the baking tray. Leave a narrow border of pastry showing. Spoon the apple mixture on top, mounding it neatly and evenly with your hands. Finally, pipe on the marzipan mixture in a zig-zag lattice pattern. Leave to stand for about 10 minutes.

Bake for 5–8 minutes or until barely golden. Leave to cool for 15 minutes, then brush with the warmed apricot jam and sprinkle with the flaked almonds. Serve at room temperature, within 24 hours. Delicious with ice-cream, cream, crème anglaise (see page 58) or fromage frais.

STRAWBERRY BABAS

Makes 12
DOUGH:
230g (8oz) unbleached white bread flour
1 teaspoon salt
15g (¹/₂oz) caster sugar
15g (¹/₂oz) fresh yeast
3 tablespoons milk, lukewarm
3 eggs, beaten
the grated rind of 1 unwaxed lemon
110g (4oz) unsalted butter, at room temperature

SYRUP:
500g (1lb 2oz) sugar
1 litre (1³/₄ pints) water
the grated rind and juice of 1 large unwaxed lemon,
    or to taste

FILLING:
250g (8³/₄oz) mascarpone or ricotta
250g (8³/₄oz) strawberries, washed and hulled
fine shreds of lemon rind for decorating (optional)

12 dariole moulds of about 125ml (4¹/₂fl oz)
    capacity, buttered (see recipe)
a baking tray

Babas are like very light sponge cakes soaked in a flavoured syrup. But, in fact, they are made from a yeast dough enriched with eggs and butter, rather than a cake mixture leavened with baking powder. Popular rum babas contain rum-soaked currants, and more rum is poured over after baking. The babas here are flavoured with lemon, and are filled before serving with mascarpone or ricotta and sliced strawberries. You could also sprinkle over a little brandy or kirsch.

To make the dough, mix the flour, salt and sugar in a mixing bowl, and make a well in the centre. Crumble the yeast into a small bowl and cream it to a smooth paste with the lukewarm milk. Pour into the well in the flour, then mix in the eggs. Work the flour into the liquids with your hand, to make a smooth, very thick, batter-like dough. Knead the dough, in the bowl, by beating it with your hand: tilt the bowl slightly and, using your hand like a spoon, lift the dough and throw it back into the bowl with a slapping motion. Continue for 5 minutes or until the dough becomes very elastic, smooth and slightly stiff. Cover the bowl with a damp tea towel and leave to rise in a warm place for 45 minutes to 1 hour or until the dough has doubled in bulk.

Butter the moulds thoroughly. Chill them in the freezer for 10 minutes and then butter them again – this doubled buttering helps prevent the delicate dough from sticking to the moulds and makes unmoulding the soft-crusted babas very easy. The butter sets, so it will not be absorbed by the dough as it rises.

Knock back the risen dough with your knuckles, then using your hand as before, beat in the grated lemon rind and the soft butter. When the mixture is very smooth, with no streaks, use two spoons to divide it among the prepared moulds. They should be just under half full. Arrange the moulds on the baking tray, cover with a damp tea towel and leave to rise at normal to warm room temperature until the dough reaches almost to the top of the moulds. This will take about 45 minutes – check to make sure the dough is not sticking to the tea towel.

1 *WHEN THOROUGHLY BEATEN, THE DOUGH WILL BE ELASTIC.*

2 *USE A PASTRY BRUSH TO COAT THE INSIDES OF THE MOULDS WITH SOFT BUTTER. CHILL AND BUTTER AGAIN.*

RIGHT The babas can be split horizontally or vertically before filling generously with creamy mascarpone and fruit.

Preheat the oven to 200C (400F, Gas 6).

Bake the babas for 15–20 minutes or until golden brown and beginning to shrink away from the sides of the moulds. Turn out very carefully on to a wire rack and leave to cool.

To make the syrup, stir the sugar and water in a saucepan over low heat until dissolved. Then bring to the boil and boil, without stirring, for 2–3 minutes or until the syrup clears. Stir in the lemon rind and juice.

Remove the pan from the heat. Add the babas, a couple at a time, to the hot syrup and leave them to soak for a minute or so, turning them over. Lift them out with a slotted spoon on to a serving plate. When cool, keep covered until ready to serve.

To make the filling, beat the mascarpone or ricotta until fluffy. Slice the strawberries and sweeten with a little sugar if necessary.

Slice off the top of each baba at an angle. Spoon a little mascarpone or ricotta on to the cut surface of each baba, then top with strawberries and replace the cut off top. Sprinkle with liqueur, if using, and shreds of lemon rind and serve as soon as possible.

NOTE To use easy-blend dried yeast instead of fresh yeast, add 1 sachet (7g/¹⁄₄oz) to the flour, salt and sugar. Proceed with the recipe, adding the lukewarm milk with the eggs.

APRICOT ALMOND PLAIT

Ideal for picnics and alfresco meals, this is a moist and fruity, well-flavoured cake made from sweet yeast dough. It is filled with chopped dried apricots and ground and chopped almonds.

Put the apricots and orange juice into a small pan. Bring to the boil, then remove from the heat and leave to soak while making and rising the sweet yeast dough.

Mix the flour and salt in a large mixing bowl. Rub in the butter to make fine crumbs. Make a well in the centre. Crumble the yeast into a small bowl and cream it to a smooth liquid with the milk. Stir in the egg. Pour the yeast mixture into the well in the flour. Gradually work the flour into the liquid to make a soft but not sticky dough. Turn the dough on to a lightly floured work surface and knead for 10 minutes or until very smooth and elastic. Return the dough to the bowl, cover with a damp tea towel and leave to rise at normal room temperature for about 1 hour or until doubled in bulk.

Meanwhile, prepare the filling. Drain the soaked apricots, reserving the liquid to glaze the baked plait. Beat the butter with the sugar until fluffy, then work in the ground almonds followed by the drained apricots, sultanas, chopped almonds and orange rind.

Knock back the risen dough with your knuckles, then turn on to a lightly floured work surface. Roll out to a rectangle about 25.5 x 30.5cm (10 x 12in). Spread the filling evenly over the dough, then roll up fairly tightly from one long side like a Swiss roll. Using your hands, gently roll the cylinder on the work surface to make it longer and thinner – it should be about 46cm (18in) long. Lift it on to the prepared baking tray.

Using a large, very sharp knife, cut the roll lengthwise into three equal strips, leaving them joined at one end. Working with the cut sides facing upwards as much as possible, plait the three strips together. Pinch the ends together and tuck under neatly. Cover loosely with a damp tea towel and leave to rise at normal room temperature for about 1 hour or until the plait has doubled in size.

Preheat the oven to 200C (400F, Gas 6).

Bake the risen plait for about 25 minutes or until golden brown and firm. Remove from the oven. Heat the reserved orange juice and brush over the hot plait. Sprinkle with the flaked almonds and transfer to a wire rack to cool. Serve warm, with cream. Eat within 2 days. To reheat the plait, wrap in foil and heat for about 10 minutes at 180C (350F, Gas 4).

INGREDIENTS

Cuts into about 8 slices
DOUGH:

230g (8oz) unbleached white bread flour
$^{1}/_{2}$ teaspoon salt
40g (1$^{1}/_{2}$oz) unsalted butter, chilled and diced
10g ($^{1}/_{4}$oz) fresh yeast
70ml (2$^{1}/_{2}$fl oz) milk, at room temperature
1 egg, beaten

FILLING:

110g (4oz) ready-to-eat dried apricots, roughly chopped
140ml (5fl oz) orange juice
85g (3oz) unsalted butter, at room temperature
60g (2oz) light muscovado sugar
30g (1oz) ground almonds
60g (2oz) sultanas
60g (2oz) blanched almonds, toasted and roughly chopped
the grated rind of 1 unwaxed orange

TO FINISH:

30g (1oz) toasted flaked almonds for sprinkling

a large baking tray, greased

NOTE To use easy-blend dried yeast instead of fresh yeast, mix 2 teaspoons with the flour and salt, then proceed with the recipe.

1 AFTER SPREADING OVER THE APRICOT FILLING, ROLL UP THE DOUGH QUITE TIGHTLY.

2 CUT THE ROLL DOWN ITS LENGTH INTO THREE STRIPS, THEN PLAIT THESE TOGETHER.

RED FRUIT SLUMP

INGREDIENTS

Serves 4
500g (1lb 2oz) fresh or frozen red fruits
3—4 tablespoons sugar, to taste
2 tablespoons water or crème de cassis

DUMPLINGS:
60g (2oz) self-raising flour
30g (1oz) unsalted butter, chilled and diced
15g (¹/₂oz) caster sugar
a pinch of ground cinnamon
2 tablespoons milk

a baking dish of about 1.15 litres (2 pints)
   capacity

This is another German dessert from Brigitte Friis (see her divine Almond Squares on page 23). A mixture of red fruits is cooked until the juices just start to run, then tiny pastry dumplings are added, and the dessert is baked until the fruit is just tender and the dumplings are cooked and feather-light. Brigitte freezes fruit from her garden – cherries, raspberries, blackberries, loganberries, strawberries and currants – to make this dessert, but the bags of mixed red fruits which are available frozen from supermarkets, and fresh fruit, work just as well.

Preheat the oven to 190C (375F, Gas 5).

Put the fruit (there is no need to thaw frozen fruit) in the baking dish and sprinkle over the sugar and the water or cassis. Cover with a lid or foil and bake in the preheated oven for 10–12 minutes or until the juices start to run – the time will depend on the type and ripeness of the fruit, and whether it is fresh or frozen.

Meanwhile, make the pastry dumplings. Sift the flour into a small mixing bowl, add the diced butter and rub in using the tips of your fingers until the mixture resembles fine crumbs. Stir in the sugar and cinnamon, and bind to a soft but not sticky dough with the milk. Using your hands, roll the mixture into 12 small balls.

Remove the baking dish from the oven, uncover and stir the fruit gently. Arrange the pastry balls in the dish so they are nestling in the hot fruit juices. Cover again and bake for about 15 minutes or until the dumplings are firm to the touch. Serve hot, warm or at room temperature, with ice-cream, cream or fromage frais.

CARROLL'S FUDGE PIE

INGREDIENTS

Serves 6–8
200g (7oz) golden caster sugar
110g (4oz) unsalted butter, at room temperature
2 eggs, separated
70g (2¹/₂oz) good dark chocolate, chopped
50g (1³/₄oz) plain flour
a few drops of pure vanilla essence
a pinch of salt

CHOCOLATE CREAM:
3 tablespoons cocoa powder
40g (1¹/₂oz) icing sugar
140ml (5fl oz) double cream, chilled
a few drops of pure vanilla essence

a 21.5cm (8¹/₂in) pie dish, about 4cm (1¹/₂in)
    deep, or tart tin (not loose-based), greased

Caroll Boltin, who makes the best brownies in the world (see the recipe on page 40), prefers this very rich chocolate pudding to Mississippi Mud Pie or Death By Chocolate. She adds that it is embarrassingly easy and quick to make for something that tastes so good. Serve in very thin slices with whipped cream, chocolate cream (recipe below) or ice-cream.

Preheat the oven to 170C (325F, Gas 3).

Beat the sugar and butter together until creamy, then beat in the egg yolks one at a time. Melt the chocolate in a heatproof bowl set over a pan of hot but not boiling water, then remove from the heat and leave to cool, stirring occasionally. Beat the cooled chocolate into the yolk mixture. Add the flour, vanilla and salt and fold into the mixture, using a large metal spoon, until thoroughly combined.

In a spotlessly clean and grease-free bowl, whisk the egg whites until stiff peaks form. Fold into the chocolate mixture in three batches.

Spoon into the prepared pie dish or tart tin and spread evenly. Bake for 30 minutes. Leave to cool and then chill.

To make the chocolate cream, sift the cocoa powder and sugar into the cream. Stir gently until combined, then cover and chill for 2 hours. The mixture should be quite stiff. Stir in the vanilla. If the cream isn't stiff, whip it until it holds its shape. The chocolate cream can also be used to sandwich chocolate macaroons or meringues (pages 24 and 41).

Decorate the fudge pie, if wished, with piped chocolate cream, or serve the cream separately.

CHAPTER THREE

BREADS & TEA LOAVES

Once you start making bread you will be absorbed by the endless variety. You will also find that working with flour, water and yeast is actually simple and straightforward — no great skill is required, only time and effort.

MY FAVOURITE BREAD

INGREDIENTS

Makes 1 large loaf
340g (12oz) unbleached white bread flour
170g (6oz) stoneground wholemeal bread flour
170g (6oz) rye flour
15g (¹/₂oz) sea salt, crushed or ground
15g (¹/₂oz) fresh yeast
430ml (15fl oz) water from the cold tap
extra flour for dusting and sprinkling

a large baking tray, lightly greased

Combining three flours — white, wholemeal and rye, all stoneground for choice — gives me the best of loaves. There is plenty of flavour, a proper crust, a good texture and chewy crumb — especially if I use coarse ground wholemeal flour — and the bread keeps well. The dough is easier to knead than a loaf made only with wholemeal flour. It is shaped into a round and simply baked on a greased baking tray, though you can also use a 900g (2lb) loaf tin.

Mix the flours and salt in a large mixing bowl and make a well in the centre. Crumble the yeast into a small bowl and cream to a smooth liquid with 4 tablespoons of the cold water. Pour the yeast liquid and the rest of the water into the well in the flour. Using your hand draw a little flour into the liquid and mix thoroughly. Gradually draw in more flour until you have a thick smooth batter in the well. Sprinkle this batter with a little flour to prevent a skin from forming, then cover the bowl with a damp tea towel and leave to 'sponge' for about 20 minutes: the batter will become aerated and frothy and will expand to fill the well in the flour. This 'sponging' shows that the yeast is not only alive and kicking but starting to grow. If the batter does not show any signs of life after 30 minutes, the yeast is probably too old and you will have to replace the yeast and liquid, and start again.

Gradually mix the remaining flour into the batter to make a firm dough. Gather the dough into a ball — it should leave the sides of the bowl clean. If the dough seems sticky or wet, work in extra flour a tablespoon at a time; if there are dry crumbs at the bottom of the bowl and the dough seems stiff, work in extra water a tablespoon at a time.

1 BREAK UP THE FRESH YEAST BY CRUMBLING IT BETWEEN YOUR FINGERS.

2 MIX THE YEAST WITH A LITTLE WATER UNTIL SMOOTH, THEN ADD TO THE FLOUR.

3 ADD THE REST OF THE WATER TO THE WELL, THEN DRAW IN THE FLOUR.

4 WHEN THE FLOUR IS MIXED IN, THE DOUGH SHOULD BE FIRM BUT NOT STICKY.

LEFT My Favourite Bread and Light Rye Loaf (see recipe on page 78).

PREVIOUS PAGE (left to right) My Favourite Bread, Simple Sourdough, Harvest Wreath, a French loaf and Light Rye Loaf.

5 IT'S IMPORTANT TO KNEAD THE DOUGH THOROUGHLY – 10 MINUTES BY HAND.

6 ROLL THE DOUGH INTO A BALL, THEN RETURN TO THE BOWL FOR THE FIRST RISE.

7 AFTER ABOUT 2 HOURS OF RISING, THE DOUGH WILL HAVE DOUBLED IN SIZE.

8 USE YOUR FIST TO FLATTEN THE DOUGH AND KNOCK OUT LARGE AIR BUBBLES.

Turn the dough on to a lightly floured work surface – use as little flour as possible – and knead it thoroughly for 10 minutes. Kneading is vital for a good even-textured loaf. It also ensures that the yeast is thoroughly distributed, so the loaf will rise and cook evenly. To knead, first stretch the dough away from you using the heel of your hand, then gather the dough back into a ball and give it a quarter turn. Continue kneading in this way by continually stretching and turning the dough; as the dough is kneaded it gradually changes texture, becoming smoother, firmer and more elastic, and looking almost glossy.

You can also use an electric mixer fitted with a dough hook to knead the dough, but as it is quite easy to over-knead using a machine – something that is almost impossible by hand – reduce the kneading time to about 7 minutes or follow the manufacturer's instructions. If the dough is over-kneaded the gluten strands that have been carefully developed and strengthened will be irretrievably broken and the dough will collapse.

I have never been able to knead a bread dough to my satisfaction in a food processor.

Shape the dough into a ball and return to the cleaned mixing bowl. (For delicate doughs I like to use a lightly greased bowl, and I turn the ball of dough over so it is covered with a thin layer of oil to prevent it from sticking or drying.) Cover the bowl with a damp tea towel, or put the bowl in a very large plastic bag that has been greased inside – a supermarket carrier bag is ideal. It is important that the dough stays moist for the yeast to work effectively; also, if a dry crust forms it can result in hard lumps in the baked loaf.

Leave the dough to rise at cool to normal room temperature, in a draught-free place, for 1½–2 hours or until doubled in bulk. Most bread recipes say to put the dough in a very warm spot so it rises very quickly, but I think bread has a better flavour if the dough is left to rise at a fairly cool temperature – around 16C (60F).

The loaf will be heavy if not left to rise for long enough, though over-rising is more of a problem: if a dough is seriously distended by being left to rise too long, it tends to collapse in the heat of the oven. If the dough is only slightly over-risen it can usually be saved if you knead it again for a couple of minutes before shaping and rising again. When the dough has properly risen you should be able to press the tip of a finger into the centre without the dough springing back.

Knock back the risen dough by flattening it with your knuckles, lightly floured. This breaks down the very large bubbles and redistributes the gases so there will be no large holes or solid pieces in the baked loaf. Turn the dough on to a floured work surface and shape it into a ball. Cup your hands, lightly floured, over the ball, then gently smooth the dough so the sides and top are nicely rounded and the ball has a good, even shape. Put the shaped loaf on to the prepared baking tray. Cover as before and leave to rise for 1½–2 hours or until doubled in size.

Preheat the oven to 220C (425F, Gas 7).

Uncover the loaf. With a very sharp knife slash the top of the dough round diagonally three times. If you wish, sprinkle with a little flour to give the surface a matt finish when baked. Bake for 15 minutes or until golden, then lower the oven temperature to 190C (375F, Gas 5) and bake for a further 20–25 minutes or until the loaf sounds hollow when tapped on the base. If it does not sound hollow, return it to the oven, placing it upside down directly on the oven rack, and bake for 5 minutes longer, then test again.

Transfer the bread to a wire rack to cool.

NOTE To use easy-blend dried yeast instead of fresh yeast, sprinkle 1 sachet (7g/¼oz) into the flours when you add the salt. Mix thoroughly. Omit the sponging stage, and mix in all the liquid at once to make the dough. Then proceed with the recipe.

9 SET THE SHAPED LOAF ON THE BAKING TRAY, COVER AND LEAVE TO RISE AGAIN.

10 THE LOAF WILL RISE TO DOUBLE IN SIZE WHILE KEEPING ITS NEAT ROUND SHAPE.

11 SLASH THE TOP OF THE LOAF WITHOUT DRAGGING THE KNIFE BLADE. BAKE.

12 HOLD THE HOT BAKED LOAF WITH A THICK CLOTH AND TAP THE UNDERSIDE.

A PLAIN WHITE LOAF

INGREDIENTS

Makes 1 large loaf
680g (1½lb) unbleached white bread flour,
  preferably stoneground
15g (½oz) sea salt, crushed or ground
15g (½oz) fresh yeast
430ml (15fl oz) water from the cold tap
extra flour for dusting

a 900g (2lb) loaf tin, greased

You can use this basic recipe to make a tin-shaped loaf, a large oval loaf, a big round or plaited loaf, or even rolls. You can also experiment with different toppings, as well as additions to the dough — sunflower or sesame seeds, chopped herbs, dried fruit and nuts, for example.

Make the dough with the flour, salt, yeast and water and knead following the instructions on pages 73-4. Cover and leave to rise until doubled in bulk.

Knock back the risen dough and turn on to a lightly floured work surface. Pat out to a rectangular shape about 2.5cm (1in) thick and the length of the tin. Roll up the dough from one short end. Pinch the seam together with your fingers, then put the dough into the prepared tin seam side down, tucking the ends underneath. The tin should be half filled. Cover the tin with a damp tea towel and leave to rise until doubled in size – about 1 hour at normal room temperature and 1½ hours in a cool room.

Preheat the oven to 230C (450F, Gas 8).

Uncover the loaf and sprinkle the top with a little flour. Using a very sharp knife, make one deep slash down the centre of the loaf. Bake for 15 minutes, then lower the oven temperature to 200C (400F, Gas 6) and bake for a further 20–30 minutes or until the loaf sounds hollow when tipped out of the tin and tapped on the base. Turn out on to a wire rack to cool.

NOTE To use easy-blend dried yeast instead of fresh yeast, add 1 sachet (7g/¼oz) to the flour and salt. Omit the sponging stage and add all the water at once. Proceed with the recipe.

1 ROLL UP THE DOUGH TIGHTLY SO THERE ARE NO LARGE AIR BUBBLES OR HOLES.

2 PINCH THE SEAM TOGETHER AND PUT INTO THE TIN, TUCKING THE ENDS UNDER.

TO SHAPE COTTAGE LOAF ROLLS (TOP), PUSH YOUR FLOURED LITTLE FINGER THROUGH THE TWO BALLS OF DOUGH. FOR OVAL ROLLS, MAKE A DEEP CREASE DOWN THE CENTRE WITH THE SIDE OF YOUR FINGER (ABOVE).

VARIATION: BREAD ROLLS Knock back the risen dough, then divide it into 60g (2oz) portions. For a *round smooth roll*, take a portion of dough and shape it into a rough ball. Cup the dough in the palm of your hand and, using the fingers of your other hand, pull the outer edge of the dough outwards then push back in towards the centre. Turn the dough and repeat until the ball is smooth and neat underneath. Another method is to put the rough ball of dough on the work surface, cup your hand over the ball so your fingertips and wrist touch the work surface, and gently rotate your hand so the dough underneath is rolled around and smoothed into a neat roll. For a *cottage loaf shape*, take a portion of dough and cut off a third. Roll each piece into a neat ball. Slightly flatten the larger ball, put the smaller ball on top and secure together by pushing a finger down through the centre. To make a *plait*, take a portion of dough and roll it into a sausage shape about 7.5cm (3in) long. Cut into three lengthways, leaving the three strands attached at one end, then plait them together. To make *wedges*, take three portions of dough and knead them together until smooth. Form into a disc about 2.5cm (1in) thick and cut this into three wedges as if cutting a cake. To make *oval rolls*, take a portion of dough and shape into a ball. Flatten slightly and mould to an oval with your hands, then make a good crease down the centre using the side of your little finger.

Arrange the rolls on greased baking trays, placing them well apart. Cover with a damp tea towel and leave to rise until doubled in size – 30–40 minutes at normal room temperature. Preheat the oven to 220C (425F, Gas 7). Remove the tea towel and lightly glaze the rolls with beaten egg or milk. Or they can be sprinkled with flour, cornmeal, sea salt, poppy seeds, rye or wheat flakes, cracked wheat or sesame seeds. Bake for 18–20 minutes or until the rolls are golden brown and sound hollow when tapped on the base.

LIGHT RYE LOAF

INGREDIENTS

Makes 1 large loaf
450g (1lb) unbleached white bread flour
230g (8oz) rye flour, stoneground if possible
1 tablespoon caraway seeds
15g (¹/₂oz) salt
15g (¹/₂oz) fresh yeast
430ml (15fl oz) water from the cold tap

a baking tray, greased

1 MAKE A DEEP CREASE IN THE CENTRE OF THE LOAF WITH THE SIDE OF YOUR HAND.

2 ROLL THE LOAF OVER AND PUT ON THE BAKING TRAY, SEAM UNDERNEATH.

Many rye breads are dark, pungent and heavy, redolent of Eastern Europe, and ideal for eating with cured fish or smoked and cured meats. They can also be light, milder, more open-textured loaves that make good toast and sandwiches. This loaf, with its high proportion of white flour, is easy to work yet has the distinct taste of rye. And, of course, caraway seeds are the perfect partner to rye.

Mix the flours, caraway seeds and salt in a large mixing bowl and make a well in the centre. Crumble the yeast into a small bowl and stir to a smooth liquid with 140ml (5fl oz) of the water. Pour the yeast liquid and the rest of the water into the well in the flour. Gradually mix in the flour to make a soft but not sticky dough. Turn the dough on to a lightly floured work surface and knead thoroughly for 10 minutes. Return the dough to the bowl, cover with a damp tea towel and leave to rise at cool to normal room temperature for about 2 hours or until doubled in bulk.

Knock back the risen dough with your knuckles, then turn it on to a lightly floured work surface. Shape into an oval by kneading it lightly. With the edge of your hand, make a good crease down the centre of the dough oval, then roll the dough over to make an oval sausage. Turn the dough over on the work surface so the seam is underneath and the top looks smooth and evenly shaped. Put the shaped loaf, seam side down, on to the prepared baking tray. Cover and leave to rise until doubled in size – about 1 hour at normal room temperature.

Preheat the oven to 220C (425F, Gas 7).

Uncover the loaf and slash it several times across the top, using a very sharp knife. Bake for 15–20 minutes or until golden, then reduce the oven temperature to 190C (375F, Gas 5) and bake for a further 20 minutes or until the loaf sounds hollow when tapped on the base. Cool on a wire rack. The loaf is best eaten within 4 days, and is also good toasted.

NOTE To use easy-blend dried yeast instead of fresh yeast, mix 1 sachet (7g/¹/₄oz) with the flours, caraway seeds and salt. Then add the water and proceed with the recipe.

Rye breads of all sizes and shapes are baked in Eastern Europe. Here, in Old Plodiv, Bulgaria, a rye dough has been made into a decorative wedding loaf.

DANISH RYE BREAD

Makes 1 large loaf
450g (1lb) rye flour
100g (3½oz) unbleached white bread flour
½ tablespoon sea salt, crushed or ground
15g (½oz) fresh yeast
140ml (5fl oz) milk, at room temperature
140ml (5fl oz) hot water
1 tablespoon black treacle or molasses
extra flour for dusting

a 900g (2lb) loaf tin, greased

David Sharland, of the Savoy Hotel in London, made this loaf for a Scandinavian festival at the hotel when he was pastry chef. He is a big fan of good rye bread, and suggests keeping this well-flavoured loaf at least a day before slicing.

Mix the flours and salt together in a large mixing bowl and make a well in the centre. Crumble the yeast into a small bowl and mix to a smooth liquid with the milk. Stir the hot water and treacle together until the treacle dissolves. Pour the yeast liquid into the well in the flour, then add the treacle liquid. Quickly mix the flour into the liquids to make a heavy sticky dough. It will be difficult to work. Because rye flour has far less gluten than wheat flour the loaf will be denser and will not rise as much as one made from all wheat flour.

Turn the dough on to a floured work surface and knead for 5 minutes – it will be hard work at first but the dough should become less sticky and more pliable. (You can always knead for a few minutes, then cover the dough and take a break for 5 minutes.) Shape the dough into a loaf to fit the tin (see page 76). Put the loaf into the prepared tin seam side down. Using a fork, prick the loaf all the way through in four or five places. Cover the tin with a damp tea towel and leave to rise at normal to warm room temperature for 2½–3 hours or until almost doubled in size.

Preheat the oven to 230C (450F, Gas 8).

Bake the loaf for 15 minutes, then lower the oven temperature to 200C (400F, Gas 6) and bake for a further 45–50 minutes or until the loaf sounds hollow when tipped out of the tin and tapped on the base. David recommends turning the loaf out of the tin about 15 minutes before the end of the baking time, and baking the loaf on the oven shelf so it will develop a good crusty finish. Transfer the cooked loaf to a wire rack to cool completely, then wrap in greaseproof paper and foil and keep for a day before eating. The bread keeps well for up to a week.

NOTE To use easy-blend dried yeast instead of fresh yeast, mix 1 sachet (7g/¼oz) with the flours, then add the milk and proceed with the recipe.

SIMPLE SOURDOUGH

Makes 1 large loaf

about 340g (12oz) bread dough (see My Favourite Bread, page 73), risen once and kept for at least 24 hours

430ml (15fl oz) water from the cold tap

15g (¹/₂oz) sea salt, crushed or ground

340g (12oz) stoneground wholemeal bread flour

about 340g (12oz) unbleached white bread flour, stoneground if possible

a baking tray, greased

Sourdough breads are fascinating to make – you never quite know if they will turn out or how they will taste. They are made from a starter dough which is either made from scratch or is a lump of dough saved from the previous loaf – plus flour, salt and water.

To make a starter from scratch, you have to make a flour and water batter and leave it to ferment for several days, during which time it absorbs the yeasts naturally present in the atmosphere. It is this fermentation that produces the appealing sour taste characteristic of this bread. The flavour of the final baked loaf depends on the pungency and quantity of the starter, as well as on the rising time. Because the flavour becomes more pronounced the longer the dough is left, you can tailor the recipe to suit your taste.

When I don't have the time to get a good sourdough starter going – and it can take 5 days – I just cut off a lump of dough from a normal yeast-raised loaf and store it in a covered bowl on the kitchen table (or in the fridge if it's hot) for at least 24 hours. I then use this as my starter. The flavour of the first loaf made this way will be quite mild. If you want to have a sourer loaf, keep the lump of dough for up to 5 days in the fridge.

Sourdough bread is usually left in a cloth-lined basket for its final rising, then inverted on to a tray for baking; however, this loaf is shaped and then risen and baked on the baking tray.

Knock down the portion of bread dough, as it will have risen even in the fridge. Put the water into a large mixing bowl, add the salt and stir until dissolved. Add the bread dough starter and mix using your hands. When the dough has broken down to make a lumpy batter full of strands and small pieces of dough, work in the wholemeal flour. When thoroughly combined, gradually work in enough white flour to make a soft but not sticky dough.

Turn the dough on to a lightly floured work surface and knead thoroughly for 10 minutes – the dough changes and becomes firmer as you knead it, so it is important not to knead in too much flour at the very beginning. Return the dough to the bowl, cover with a damp tea towel and

1 USE YOUR HANDS TO SQUEEZE AND MIX THE DOUGH STARTER INTO THE SALT WATER.

2 CONTINUE MIXING VIGOROUSLY TO BREAK DOWN THE DOUGH AND MAKE A LUMPY BATTER.

3 WORK IN THE WHOLEMEAL FLOUR. THE DOUGH WILL BE SMOOTH BUT STICKY.

4 ADD ENOUGH WHITE FLOUR TO MAKE A SOFT DOUGH THAT IS NO LONGER STICKY.

leave to rise until almost doubled in bulk. In a cool room this will take around 12 hours, or 8 hours at normal room temperature.

Knock down the risen dough with your knuckles. Turn on to a lightly floured work surface and cut off a portion – about 340g (12oz) – to keep as the starter for the next loaf. Cover and store this starter in the fridge for up to 5 days. Shape the rest of the dough into a round or oval loaf (see page 75 or 78). If the dough seems at all sticky or very soft, work in a little more flour, otherwise the loaf won't hold its shape during baking.

Put the loaf on to the prepared baking tray, then cover and leave to rise as before until almost doubled in size – 8 hours in a cool room, 4 hours at normal room temperature.

Preheat the oven to 225C (450F, Gas 8).

Slash the top of the loaf several times, using a very sharp knife. Bake for 20 minutes, then reduce the oven temperature to 200C (400F, Gas 6) and bake for a further 15 minutes or until the loaf sounds hollow when tapped on the base. Transfer to a wire rack to cool.

The loaf will keep well for at least 5 days, and, when no longer at the peak of freshness, makes wonderful toast.

ORANGE PUMPERNICKEL BREAD

Makes 2 small loaves

280g (10oz) rye flour, preferably coarse
  stoneground

170g (6oz) unbleached white bread flour

110g (4oz) stoneground wholemeal bread flour

2 teaspoons salt

15g (1/2oz) fresh yeast

340ml (12fl oz) lukewarm water

2 tablespoons light muscovado sugar

85g (3oz) molasses

1 tablespoon vegetable oil, or 15g (1/2oz) butter,
  melted

the grated rind of 1 unwaxed orange

85g (3oz) raisins

two 450g (1lb) loaf tins, greased

You can't buy pumpernickel flour — pumpernickel bread is made from a blend of several flours and grains. It always contains a fair proportion of rye flour, which accounts for its dense texture and strong flavour. Commercial loaves are often baked for several hours in a slightly steamy oven, which helps develop the dark rich colour. This slightly sweet loaf is excellent with creamy cheeses and makes good open sandwiches — we enjoyed something very similar at the Rose Garden tea restaurant at the Huntington Botanical Gardens in Pasadena, California. Pumpernickel bread is also fine toasted and spread with butter and marmalade for breakfast.

Mix the three flours and salt together in a large mixing bowl and make a well in the centre. Crumble the yeast into a small bowl and stir it to a smooth liquid with the water. Pour the yeast liquid into the well in the flour, followed by the sugar, molasses and oil or butter. Mix together all the ingredients in the well, then work in the flour to make a soft and slightly sticky dough – it will be heavy and quite difficult to work.

1 COMBINE THE THREE FLOURS IN A BOWL, MIX TOGETHER AND MAKE A WELL IN THE CENTRE.

2 MIX THE YEAST LIQUID, SUGAR, MOLASSES AND OIL TOGETHER IN THE WELL.

3 AFTER RISING, ADD THE RAISINS AND GRATED ORANGE RIND TO THE DOUGH AND KNEAD IN.

Turn the dough on to a lightly floured work surface and knead for 10 minutes. The dough will still be heavy but will have become firmer and more elastic. If you find the kneading hard work, cover the dough with the up-turned mixing bowl and take a breather for a few minutes before continuing. Return the kneaded dough to the bowl, cover with a damp tea towel and leave to rise until doubled in bulk – about 3 hours at normal room temperature.

Knock back the risen dough with your knuckles, then turn it on to a lightly floured work surface. Sprinkle the orange rind and raisins over the dough and knead for a minute until evenly distributed. Divide the dough in half and shape each piece into a loaf to fit the tins (see page 76). Put into the prepared tins seam side down. Cover with a damp tea towel and leave to rise until doubled in size: $1\frac{1}{2}$–2 hours at room temperature.

Preheat the oven to 200C (400F, Gas 6).

Bake the risen loaves for 35–40 minutes or until they sound hollow when tipped out of the tin and tapped on the base. Turn out on to a wire rack to cool. When cold, wrap in greaseproof paper, then in foil. Keep for a day before slicing.

ITALIAN SEMOLINA BREAD

Makes 1 large loaf

15g (¹/₂oz) fresh yeast

115ml (4fl oz) water from the cold tap

200g (7oz) unbleached white bread flour

280g (10oz) semolina flour

1 teaspoon salt

30g (1oz) butter, chilled and diced

1 tablespoon honey

1 egg, beaten

beaten egg for glazing

a baking tray, greased

Durum wheat semolina flour, the kind used for pasta, makes a good textured, fairly close loaf with a nice flavour. Because the flour is hard, with a higher gluten content than even strong bread flour, I think it is best to mix it with white or wholemeal bread flour to prevent the loaf from being tough. Good Italian delis should stock semolina flour.

Crumble the yeast into a small bowl and mix to a smooth liquid with the water. Mix the flours and salt together in a large mixing bowl. Add the diced butter and rub in using the tips of your fingers to make fine crumbs. Stir the honey and egg into the yeast liquid, then add to the flour mixture and mix to a soft but not sticky dough.

Turn on to a lightly floured work surface and knead thoroughly for 10 minutes. Shape the dough into a ball, return it to the bowl and cover. Leave to rise at normal room temperature for 1–1¹/₂ hours or until the dough has doubled in bulk.

Knock back the risen dough with your knuckles and turn it on to a very lightly floured work surface. Shape the dough into an oval (see page 78) and place on the prepared baking tray. Cover with a damp tea towel and leave to rise as before until doubled in size – about 1 hour.

Preheat the oven to 190C (375F, Gas 5).

Brush the risen loaf with beaten egg to glaze, then bake for 30–35 minutes or until the bread sounds hollow when tapped on the base. Transfer to a wire rack to cool. Eat within 24 hours, or toast, or freeze for up to 3 months.

NOTE To use easy-blend dried yeast instead of fresh yeast, mix 1 sachet (7g/¹/₄oz) with the flours and salt. Rub in the butter. Mix the water with the honey and egg. Proceed with the recipe.

OPPOSITE Eating al fresco at Paghezzana, Italy.

EASTER BRAID

INGREDIENTS

Makes 1 large loaf

680g (1½lb) unbleached white bread flour

60g (2oz) caster sugar

2 teaspoons salt

1 tablespoon ground mixed spice

15g (½oz) fresh yeast

430ml (15fl oz) lukewarm milk

85g (3oz) unsalted butter, chilled and diced

1 egg, beaten

110g (4oz) currants

30g (1oz) mixed candied peel, finely chopped

GLAZE:

beaten egg for brushing

about 3 tablespoons honey, warmed

a large baking tray, lightly greased

Here the dough traditionally used for Hot Cross Buns — rich with butter, spice and fruit — is plaited into an attractive loaf and glazed with honey. To keep its shape, the dough should not be too soft, and should not be left to rise in a warm spot. Left-over Braid is excellent toasted or used for Bread and Butter Pudding (see page 52).

Put about 170g (6oz) of the flour into a small mixing bowl with the sugar, and make a well in the centre. Sift the remaining flour with the salt and spice into a large mixing bowl. Crumble the yeast into the well in the smaller bowl. Pour the lukewarm milk on to the yeast and mix until combined. Work the flour and sugar into the yeast liquid to make a smooth batter. Cover and leave to 'sponge' for about 20 minutes – the batter will become bubbly as the yeast begins to grow.

Add the diced butter to the flour mixture in the larger bowl and rub in using your fingertips until the mixture looks like coarse crumbs. Stir the egg into the frothy yeast batter and add to the flour. Mix together to form a fairly firm, rather than soft or sticky, dough. Turn the dough on to a lightly floured work surface and knead for 10 minutes or until quite firm, silky smooth and elastic. Put the dough back into the bowl, cover with a damp tea towel and leave to rise at cool to normal room temperature for 1–1½ hours or until doubled in bulk.

Turn the risen dough on to a lightly floured work surface and knock back with your knuckles. Sprinkle over the currants and peel, and gently but thoroughly knead into the dough until evenly distributed. The dough should be quite pliable but not soft, and it should hold its shape well. If not, work in a little more flour. Weigh the dough and divide into three equal pieces.

Using your hands, roll each piece into a sausage shape about 40cm (16in) long. Lay the three pieces of dough parallel to each other on the prepared baking tray, then plait them together neatly but not too tightly. Take care not to stretch the dough unduly. Tuck the ends under. Cover with a damp tea towel and leave to rise at cool to normal room temperature for about 1 hour or until almost doubled in size.

Preheat the oven to 220C (425F, Gas 7).

1 ROLL EACH OF THE THREE PIECES OF DOUGH INTO A LONG, EVEN SAUSAGE SHAPE.

2 LAY THE PIECES ON THE BAKING TRAY AND PLAIT WITHOUT STRETCHING THE DOUGH.

3 TUCK UNDER THE ENDS OF THE FINISHED PLAIT, THEN LEAVE TO RISE BEFORE BAKING.

Carefully brush the loaf with the beaten egg, then bake for 15–20 minutes or until golden. Lower the oven temperature to 200C (400F, Gas 6) and bake for a further 20 minutes or until the loaf sounds hollow when tapped on the base. Transfer to a wire rack and brush with the warm honey. Leave to cool.

NOTE To use easy-blend dried yeast instead of fresh yeast, add 1 sachet (7g/¼oz) to the 170g (6oz) flour and sugar. Pour the measured lukewarm milk into the well and proceed with the recipe.

HARVEST WREATH

INGREDIENTS

Makes 1 large wreath

900g (2lb) unbleached white bread flour,
   preferably stoneground

1¹/₂ tablespoons salt

15g (¹/₂oz) fresh yeast

570ml (1 pint) water from the cold tap

1 egg, beaten with a large pinch of salt, for glazing

a large baking tray, greased

As Anthony and I travelled though Europe, we came across many extremely attractive loaves baked to celebrate the harvest. This elaborately decorated loaf was made to eat at a party in a Burgundy vineyard at the end of the vendange, or grape-picking. There is a fair amount of salt in the dough, which enables it to maintain its shape. As with the Easter Braid on page 86, it is important that the dough is smooth but not soft and that it is left to rise in a fairly cool spot.

Put the flour and salt into a large mixing bowl and make a well in the centre. Crumble the yeast into a small bowl, add a quarter of the water and mix to a smooth liquid. Pour into the well in the flour, then add the rest of the water. Gradually mix the flour into the liquid to make a fairly firm dough. Turn the dough on to a lightly floured work surface and knead thoroughly for 10 minutes – the dough must be smooth and pliable. If it is at all sticky, knead in extra flour a tablespoon at a time. Put the dough back into the bowl, cover with a damp tea towel and leave to rise at cool to normal room temperature for 1¹/₂–2 hours or until doubled in bulk.

Knock back the risen dough with your knuckles. Weigh the dough and divide into four equal portions. Cover and set aside one portion of the dough to be used for decoration. Using your hands, roll each of the remaining three portions into a sausage shape about 61cm (24in) long. Lay the three sausages parallel to each other on the work surface and hold one end of each together in one hand. With the other hand lift and twist the three strands together. Carefully join both ends of the twisted dough together to make a neat wreath. Transfer to the prepared baking tray.

1 USE BOTH HANDS TO TWIST THE STRANDS OF DOUGH TOGETHER WITHOUT STRETCHING.

2 JOIN THE ENDS TO MAKE A CIRCLE, LIFT IT ON TO THE BAKING TRAY AND NEATEN THE EDGES.

3 ROLL OUT THE REST OF THE DOUGH THINLY AND CUT OUT 9 LEAF SHAPES WITH A KNIFE.

4 TO MAKE THE GRAPES ROLL THE LEFT-OVER DOUGH INTO BALLS OF DIFFERENT SIZES.

Decorating the Harvest Wreath takes time, and a second pair of hands will be welcome. Here Anthony and I present our loaf, ready for baking.

Preheat the oven to 220C (425F, Gas 7).

Turn the reserved piece of dough on to a lightly floured work surface and knock back with your knuckles. Roll it out about 6mm (¼in) thick. Then, using a very sharp knife and a real vine leaf or a paper template as a guide, cut out nine vine leaves. Use the left-over dough to make grapes the size of hazelnuts and small peas.

Attach the vine leaves and grapes in bunches to the wreath, using the egg glaze as a glue. Brush the decorated wreath all over with more egg glaze, then bake immediately in the preheated oven for 30–40 minutes or until the bread sounds hollow when tapped on the base. If the wreath seems to be browning very rapidly, reduce the oven temperature to 200C (400F, Gas 6). Check the wreath several times during baking to ensure that it is browning evenly, and turn it as necessary. To make sure the decorations remain in place, you may need to stick them back with more egg glaze during baking. Cool the wreath on a wire rack, and eat within 24 hours.

NOTE To use easy-blend dried yeast instead of fresh yeast, mix 1 sachet (7g/¼oz) with the flour. Add all the water and proceed with the recipe.

BRIOCHE

INGREDIENTS

Makes 1 large or 2 medium brioches or
    20 small brioches
15g (¹/₂oz) fresh yeast
70ml (2¹/₂fl oz) lukewarm milk
15g (¹/₂oz) salt
500g (1lb 2oz) unbleached white bread flour
6 eggs, beaten
250g (8³/₄oz) unsalted butter, at room temperature
60g (2oz) caster sugar
110g (4oz) raisins, or good dark chocolate, chopped
    (optional)
1 egg, lightly beaten, for glazing

a large brioche mould, 24cm (9¹/₂in) wide at the
    top, or a 900g (2lb) loaf tin, greased (see
    recipe) OR two medium brioche moulds,
    16.5cm (6¹/₂in) wide at the top, or two 450g
    (1lb) loaf tins, greased OR 20 small brioche
    moulds 8cm (3¹/₂in) wide at the top, greased

With its slightly sweet, luxuriously buttery taste and fine sponge-like crumb, the brioche is half way between bread and cake. It is delicious eaten warm with butter for breakfast or tea. The fine texture of the crumb is achieved by using good fresh unsalted butter and by giving the dough three risings. Two of these should be at normal room temperature — too warm and the butter will melt and ooze out of the dough; the other rising is in the fridge to make the soft rich dough firm enough to maintain its shape. The dough can be left plain, or flavoured with raisins and grated orange rind or with chunks of the best chocolate.

Here I've adapted the best recipe I know for brioche: it comes from the Michelin Three Star chef, Michel Roux, and uses an electric mixer to cut out the hard work.

Crumble the yeast into the warm milk and pour into the bowl of an electric mixer fitted with a dough hook. Add the salt, flour and eggs, and mix to a soft dough. Then knead, still using the dough hook, for about 10 minutes or until the dough is smooth and elastic. Alternatively, you can combine all the ingredients in a large mixing bowl and knead the dough

1 MIX THE YEAST LIQUID, SALT, FLOUR AND BEATEN EGGS INTO A SOFT DOUGH.

2 AFTER BEATING IN THE BUTTER AND SUGAR, THE DOUGH WILL BE GLOSSY AND ELASTIC.

3 FLOUR YOUR KNUCKLES AND PUNCH THE CENTRE OF THE RISEN DOUGH.

4 MAKE A HOLE IN THE CENTRE OF THE DOUGH BALL TO HOLD THE SHAPED 'TOPKNOT'.

5 AFTER THE SECOND RISE, GLAZE THE BRIOCHE WITH BEATEN EGG AND THEN BAKE.

by hand, by beating and slapping the dough up and down in the bowl. This will take 15–20 minutes – the dough is ready when it comes away from the sides of the bowl in one piece.

In another bowl, beat the soft butter and sugar together until light and fluffy. With the electric mixer on low speed, add the butter mixture to the dough a little at a time, making sure each addition is completely amalgamated before adding more. If you are working by hand, squeeze the butter into the dough. Continue to beat for a couple of minutes in the mixer, or 5 minutes by hand, until the dough is smooth, glossy and elastic. Cover the bowl with a damp tea towel and leave to rise at normal to warm room temperature (no more than 22C, 72F) for about 2 hours or until doubled in bulk.

Knock back the risen dough in the bowl, using floured knuckles, then cover as before and put into the refrigerator. Leave to chill for several hours but not more than a day.

Turn the dough on to a lightly floured work surface. Sprinkle over the raisins or chopped chocolate, if using, and briefly and gently knead in until evenly distributed. Shape the dough into a large ball.

Prepare the moulds or tins: brush with a thin layer of melted butter, then chill until the butter hardens. Brush with a second coat of melted butter and chill briefly. By greasing the mould in this way the butter will not be absorbed by the dough, but it will help to prevent the brioche from sticking during baking.

To make a large brioche in the brioche mould, cut off a quarter of the dough for the top and set aside. Shape the larger piece of dough into a ball and place it in the prepared mould. Make a hole in the centre with your fingertips. Roll the small piece of dough into an elongated egg shape with your hand held at an angle against the work surface. Using floured fingertips, gently press the narrow end of the dough 'egg' into the hole in the large ball. If you are using a loaf tin, shape the dough following the method on page 76.

If making two medium brioches, divide the dough into two equal portions, then shape each as for the large brioche. For small individual brioches, divide the dough into 20 equal portions and shape each as for the large brioche.

Place the mould(s) or tin(s) in a large plastic bag that has been lightly greased inside, and fasten. Leave to rise at normal room temperature for 1–1½ hours or until almost doubled in size.

Preheat the oven to 220C (425F, Gas 7).

Lightly brush the top of the brioche(s) with the egg glaze, working from the outside inwards. Take care not to let any glaze run into the crack between the large ball of dough and the top or on to the edges of the mould as this would prevent the dough from rising properly. Bake the brioche(s) in the preheated oven until golden brown and they sound hollow when tipped out of the mould or tin and tapped on the base. The large brioche will take 40–45 minutes; the medium brioches will take 25–30 minutes; and the small brioches 8–10 minutes. Turn out immediately on to a wire rack and leave to cool.

NOTE To use easy-blend dried yeast instead of fresh yeast, add 1 sachet (7g/¼oz) to the flour and proceed with the recipe.

TIPSY PRUNE FRIENDSHIP CAKE

INGREDIENTS

Makes 1 large loaf
STARTER:
280g (10oz) plain flour
15g (1/2oz) fresh yeast
455ml (16fl oz) water, at room temperature

FOR DAY 1:
200g (7oz) caster sugar
140g (5oz) plain flour
230ml (8fl oz) milk, at room temperature

FOR DAY 5:
200g (7oz) caster sugar
140g (5oz) plain flour
230ml (8fl oz) milk, at room temperature

FOR DAY 10, FINISHING THE LOAF:
250g (8³/₄oz) stoned ready-to-eat prunes, roughly
    chopped
the grated rind and juice of 1 unwaxed orange
1¹/₂ tablespoons orange liqueur
200g (7oz) light muscovado sugar
280g (10oz) plain flour
115ml (4fl oz) vegetable oil
¹/₄ teaspoon salt
2 teaspoons baking powder
2 eggs, beaten

TOPPING:
85g (3oz) dark muscovado sugar
30g (1oz) unsalted butter, at room
    temperature

a 23 x 32.5cm (9 x 13in) cake tin or roasting
    tin, greased

This is such an odd recipe – a fruit-filled sourdough loaf cake – but one I'm always asked for when I do demonstrations or radio phone-in programmes. I believe the recipe originated in Germany in the days before cakes were made with baking powder, but I've eaten it in Amish and German communities in America, and at church suppers here. It is simple to make but takes 13 days for the dough to ferment. However, you will eventually have enough starter to bake your cake plus one to keep for your next cake and two portions to give away. A couple of years ago I gave a portion of starter to Joy Skipper, who assisted on this and The Bread Book, and she has made a friendship cake every fortnight since, experimenting with different fillings. This is her favourite.

To make the starter, put the flour in a large, non-metallic bowl and make a well in the centre. Crumble the fresh yeast into the well, then pour in the water and stir using a wooden spoon until the yeast has mixed smoothly with the liquid. Gradually stir in the flour to make a sticky batter. Cover the bowl with a damp tea towel. Leave it on the kitchen table or work surface so the batter can absorb extra yeasts from the air. It's a good idea to make a note of the day or date because it is only too easy to lose your place in the recipe. Stir the batter once a day for each of the next 3 days, and re-dampen the towel each day. At the end of this time, the starter will be ready to use.

To make the dough, stir the starter you have made, or any starter you have been given, and proceed as follows:
DAY 1: Stir the starter and add the sugar, flour and milk. Stir well to mix, then cover with a damp tea towel and leave overnight at room temperature.
DAY 2: Stir well and re-cover with a damp tea towel.
DAYS 3 and 4: Do nothing but re-dampen the towel each day.
DAY 5: Stir well and add the sugar, flour and milk. Stir well again, cover with a damp tea towel and leave overnight at room temperature as before.
DAY 6: Stir well and re-cover with a damp tea towel.
DAYS 7, 8 and 9: Do nothing but re-dampen the towel each day.
DAY 10: Stir well, then divide the starter dough into four equal portions. Give two portions to friends, with instructions, keep one portion for your next batch (see below), and use one portion to make the loaf.

To make the loaf, put the chopped prunes into a mixing bowl with the grated orange rind and juice and the liqueur. Cover tightly and leave to soak for several hours or overnight.

Preheat the oven to 180C (350F, Gas 4).

Add the portion of starter dough to the prunes, together with the sugar, flour, oil, salt, baking powder and eggs. Using a wooden spoon, mix until thoroughly combined. Spoon into the prepared tin and level the surface. Sprinkle the dark muscovado sugar over the top and dot with small flakes of the butter. Bake for 30–40 minutes or until a skewer inserted into the centre comes out clean. Turn out on to a wire rack to cool.

Serve cut into squares or fingers. The cake is also good eaten warm with custard as a pudding. Eat within 3 days of baking.

NOTE To keep the portion of starter for your next cake, add 1 teaspoon of sugar and stir well, then store in a covered container in the fridge for up to 1 week. To make a fresh cake begin at Day 1 using this starter.

VARIATION Put the portion of starter into a bowl and mix in 200g (7oz) light muscovado sugar, 85g (3oz) sultanas, 280g (10oz) plain flour, 110ml (4fl oz) vegetable oil, 60g (2oz) walnut halves, ½ teaspoon salt, 2 teaspoons each ground cinnamon and baking powder, 2 eggs and 2 cooking apples, peeled, cored and diced. Put the dough into the prepared tin and add the topping as given. Bake as above.

KULICH

INGREDIENTS

Makes 1 loaf

85g (3oz) sultanas

1 tablespoon rum

a large pinch of saffron threads

230ml (8fl oz) milk, heated to boiling

85g (3oz) whole blanched almonds

60g (2oz) mixed candied orange and lemon peel,
    finely chopped

1 teaspoon plain flour

140g (5oz) unsalted butter, at room temperature

110g (4oz) icing sugar, sifted

6 egg yolks

½ teaspoon salt

30g (1oz) fresh yeast

450g (1lb) unbleached white bread flour

a 15cm (6in) round deep cake tin, greased and
    prepared with foil and greaseproof paper (see
    recipe)

a baking tray

This light fruit loaf is made in Russia to celebrate Easter, and contains all the eggs and butter prohibited during Lent. In some parts of Russia, the loaf is covered with a thin, lemony glacé icing and decorated with glacé fruits, but I have left this version plain. Kulich is traditionally eaten with paskha, a sweetened and decorated fruit, nut and curd cheese dessert made in a similar tall mould. As tall narrow moulds are hard to find, some cooks use coffee tins or well-seasoned flower pots; however, I find these more trouble than they are worth and instead use a small, deep cake tin with a stiff foil collar to extend the depth.

To prepare the tin, wrap a doubled strip of foil around the outside of the greased tin to extend about 10cm (4in) above the rim. Tie on the foil collar securely. Butter a strip of greaseproof paper and use to line the inside of the tin sides and the foil collar.

Preheat the oven to 200C (400F, Gas 6).

Put the sultanas to soak in the rum. Crumble the saffron into a small mixing bowl and pour over the boiling milk. Leave to infuse for 30 minutes – longer if possible. Put the almonds in a small mixing bowl, add enough hot water to cover and leave to soak for 5 minutes. Then drain and cut lengthwise into slivers. Arrange the almonds in a single layer on the baking tray and toast in the oven for 5–10 minutes or until lightly browned. Leave to cool. Toss the candied peel with the teaspoon of flour.

Cream the butter with the sugar in a large mixing bowl, using an electric mixer or wooden spoon. When the mixture is light and fluffy, beat in the egg yolks one at a time followed by the salt. If necessary, gently warm the saffron milk until it is just lukewarm, then crumble in the yeast and stir until smooth. Add the flour to the creamed mixture and stir until just combined, then pour in the yeast liquid. Beat with your hand for about 8 minutes or until the mixture comes together to make a very soft, smooth, cake-like dough. Cover the bowl with a damp tea towel and leave to rise at normal to warm room temperature for about 2 hours or until doubled in bulk.

Knock back the risen dough. Sprinkle it with the soaked sultanas, the candied peel and the toasted almonds. Gently work them into the dough with your hands until evenly distibuted. Spoon the dough into the prepared tin; it will be about half full. Cover with a damp tea towel and leave to rise at normal to warm room temperature for about 1½ hours or until risen almost to the top of the foil and paper collar.

Preheat the oven to 200C (400F, Gas 6) again.

Bake the kulich for 20 minutes or until starting to colour, then reduce the oven temperature to 180C (350F, Gas 4) and bake for a further 45–55 minutes or until a skewer inserted into the centre comes out clean. If the loaf starts to turn dark brown, cover with a sheet of foil or greaseproof paper. Put the tin on a wire rack and leave to cool for 10–15 minutes or until the kulich is firm enough to unmould, then turn it out on to a wire rack to cool completely. Best eaten within 3 days.

NOTE To use easy-blend dried yeast instead of fresh yeast, mix 2 sachets (7g/¼oz each) with the flour, then proceed with the recipe.

1 AFTER ADDING THE FLOUR TO THE CREAMED MIXTURE, POUR IN THE WARM YEAST LIQUID.

2 BEAT THE MIXTURE WITH YOUR HAND, LIFTING IT AND SLAPPING IT DOWN.

3 AFTER RISING, ADD THE FRUIT, PEEL AND NUTS TO THE DOUGH AND WORK THEM IN.

4 TRANSFER THE DOUGH TO THE TIN, PREPARED WITH A STIFF FOIL COLLAR.

TEA BREAD

This is an old-fashioned recipe where the dried fruit is soaked in good strong tea before it is mixed into a sweet and spicy yeasted bread dough. I am very fond of this bread sliced and buttered with afternoon tea in summer, and toasted on an open fire in winter. It also makes a jolly good Bread and Butter Pudding (see page 52).

Put the dried fruit and peel into a mixing bowl and pour over the hot tea. Mix well and leave to soak for 1 hour.

Drain the fruit in a sieve set over a measuring jug. Make the liquid up to 280ml (10fl oz) with the milk. Crumble the yeast into the liquid and stir until smooth and thoroughly mixed.

Mix the flour with the salt, mixed spice and sugar in a large mixing bowl. Add the diced butter and rub in using the tips of your fingers until the mixture looks like fine crumbs. Stir in the drained fruit, then make a well in the centre of the mixture. Pour the yeast liquid into this well. Gradually mix the flour into the liquid to make a soft dough.

Turn the dough on to a lightly floured work surface and knead for 10 minutes or until the dough is elastic and not sticky. It does not matter if the fruit bursts open – in fact it will taste better. Return the dough to the bowl, cover with a damp tea towel and leave to rise at normal room temperature for about 1½ hours or until doubled in bulk.

Gently knock back the risen dough with your knuckles, then turn on to a lightly floured work surface. Shape into a loaf to fit the tin (see page 76). Put the loaf into the prepared tin, seam side down, then cover and leave to rise for about 45 minutes or until doubled in size.

Preheat the oven to 200C (400F, Gas 6).

Brush the loaf with milk, then bake for 35–40 minutes or until nicely browned and the loaf sounds hollow when carefully tipped out of the tin and tapped on the base. Turn out on to a wire rack and leave to cool. Eat sliced and buttered or toasted.

VARIATION: STICKY FRUIT BUNS Prepare the dough and leave to rise as above. Knock back the risen dough, then divide into 8 equal pieces. Shape each into a ball and place them, well apart, on two greased baking trays. Cover and leave to rise as above. Bake for about 20 minutes or until golden brown and puffed up. Remove from the oven and immediately brush with a hot sticky glaze made by dissolving 3 tablespoons caster sugar in 3 tablespoons whole milk. Transfer the buns to a wire rack and leave to cool completely.

INGREDIENTS

Makes 1 large loaf

110g (4oz) mixed dried fruit and chopped candied
    peel
140ml (5fl oz) strong hot tea, strained
about 170ml (6fl oz) milk, at room temperature
15g (¹/₂oz) fresh yeast
450g (1lb) unbleached white bread flour
1 teaspoon salt
1 teaspoon ground mixed spice
30g (1oz) caster sugar
60g (2oz) butter, chilled and diced
milk for brushing

a 900g (2lb) loaf tin, greased

NOTE To use easy-blend dried yeast instead of fresh yeast, mix 1 sachet (7g/¹/₄oz) into the flour with the sugar, salt and spice. Proceed with the recipe, adding the tea and milk liquid to the well in the flour.

1 TO SHAPE BUNS, CUP A PIECE OF DOUGH IN ONE HAND AND PULL THE SIDES ON TO THE TOP.

2 PINCH THE TOP TOGETHER. TURN THE BUN OVER SO THE SMOOTH SIDE IS UPPERMOST.

LEMON DRIZZLE LOAF

INGREDIENTS

Makes 1 large loaf
170g (6oz) unsalted butter, at room temperature
255g (9oz) golden caster sugar
255g (9oz) self-raising flour
3 eggs, beaten
115ml (4fl oz) whole milk
the grated rind of 3 unwaxed lemons

TOPPING:
the juice of 2 lemons
the grated rind of 1 unwaxed lemon
110g (4oz) golden caster sugar

a 900g (2lb) loaf tin, greased and lined on the
   bottom

*ABOVE (left to right): Tea Bread, Sticky Fruit
Buns and Lemon Drizzle Loaf.*

The all-in-one method of making a cake, where all the ingredients — usually flour, butter, eggs and sugar — are dumped into a mixing bowl and beaten to a smooth thick batter, is reckoned to be idiot proof. Indeed, I was able to turn out something edible while only four foot high. I think this method is best reserved for loaf cakes, such as the one here, where taste and moistness are more important than lightness and volume.

If possible, use unwaxed fruit in this plain but intensely flavoured loaf. If the fruit has been waxed, be sure to scrub it well with hot soapy water and then rinse thoroughly. Serve with tea or coffee, for a simple dessert with ice cream, or hot out of the oven with custard.

Preheat the oven to 180C (350F, Gas 4).

Put all the ingredients, except those for the topping, into a large mixing bowl. Using an electric mixer or wooden spoon, beat until thick and fluffy with no sign of lumps or streaks of flour. Spoon into the prepared tin and smooth the surface. Bake in the preheated oven for 50–55 minutes or until a skewer or cocktail stick inserted into the centre comes out clean.

While the loaf is baking, combine all the ingredients for the topping. As soon as the loaf is cooked, remove it from the oven but leave it in the tin. Prick it all over with a cocktail stick or skewer. Quickly spoon over the topping mixture, then leave the loaf to cool completely before turning out. Serve thickly sliced.

NUT AND RAISIN BREAD

INGREDIENTS

Makes 2 medium loaves

450g (1lb) stoneground wholemeal bread flour

230g (8oz) unbleached white bread flour

2¹/₂ teaspoons salt

15g (¹/₂oz) fresh yeast

340ml (12fl oz) water from the cold tap

1¹/₂ tablespoons well-flavoured honey

extra flour for dusting

170g (6oz) large seedless raisins

170g (6oz) walnuts, hazelnuts or a mixture, toasted and roughly chopped

2 baking trays, greased

NOTE To use easy-blend dried yeast instead of fresh yeast, mix 1 sachet (7g/¹/₄oz) with the flour and salt. Omit the sponging stage, adding the water all at once. Proceed with the recipe.

VARIATIONS: PECAN BREAD Use 340g (12oz) each stoneground wholemeal bread flour and unbleached white bread flour, and make the dough as above. Replace the raisins and nuts with 230g (8oz) roughly chopped but untoasted pecans, then proceed with the recipe.

WALNUT OR MIXED NUT BREAD Make the dough, then knead in either 230g (8oz) toasted walnut halves or 280g (10oz) toasted and roughly chopped mixed nuts such as walnuts, hazelnuts, almonds, pecans, cashews and macadamias. Proceed with the recipe.

Lightly toasting walnuts and hazelnuts in the oven intensifies their rich taste. Combined with the largest, most luscious raisins available, they make a wonderfully flavoured loaf that's good simply sliced and buttered or served with cheese.

Mix the flours and salt together in a large mixing bowl and make a well in the centre. Crumble the yeast into a small bowl and cream it to a smooth liquid with half of the water and the honey. Pour the yeast liquid into the well in the flour and mix in just enough of the flour to make a thick batter. Leave to 'sponge' for about 15 minutes – it will look bubbly.

Add the remaining cold water to the yeast batter, then gradually work in the rest of the flour to make a soft but not sticky dough. If the dough sticks to your fingers work in a little extra flour a tablespoon at a time. If dry crumbs form and the dough seems stiff and hard to bring together, work in a little extra water a tablespoon at a time.

Turn the dough on to a lightly floured work surface and knead for 10 minutes or until smooth and elastic. Sprinkle the raisins and nuts over the dough and knead them in gently until they are evenly distributed – this will take about 2 minutes.

Shape the dough into a ball and return it to the bowl. Cover with a damp tea towel and leave to rise at cool to normal room temperature for about 2 hours or until doubled in bulk.

Knock back the risen dough with your knuckles, then turn on to a floured work surface and knead for a minute. Divide the dough in half and shape each portion into a neat ball. Place on the prepared baking trays, cover as before and leave to rise at normal room temperature for about 1¹/₂ hours or until doubled in size.

Preheat the oven to 220C (425F, Gas 7).

Slash the top of each loaf two or three times using a very, very sharp knife. Bake for 15 minutes, then reduce the oven temperature to 190C (375F, Gas 5) and bake for a further 20–25 minutes or until the loaves sound hollow when tipped off the trays and tapped on the base. Transfer to a wire rack to cool completely.

Eat the bread within 3 days, or toast, or freeze for up to a month.

STEM GINGER GINGERBREAD

INGREDIENTS

Makes 1 large loaf

230g (8oz) self-raising flour

1 teaspoon bicarbonate of soda

1 tablespoon ground ginger

1 teaspoon ground cinnamon

1 teaspoon ground mixed spice

110g (4oz) unsalted butter, chilled and diced

110g (4oz) black treacle or molasses

110g (4oz) golden syrup

110g (4oz) light or dark muscovado sugar

280ml (10fl oz) milk

45g (1½oz) drained stem ginger, grated

1 egg, size 1, beaten (or use 2 eggs, size 3)

a 900g (2lb) loaf tin, greased and lined on the bottom

A lovely spicy, sticky gingerbread, nicely hot with chopped stem ginger. I like it thickly sliced and buttered, but Anthony prefers it with a slice of moist, slightly acidic Lancashire cheese.

Preheat the oven to 180C (350F, Gas 4).

Sift the flour, bicarbonate of soda and all the spices into a large mixing bowl. Add the diced butter and rub in with your fingertips until the mixture resembles fine crumbs.

In a small saucepan, melt the treacle with the syrup, then leave to cool to blood heat. Meanwhile, in another small pan, dissolve the sugar in the milk over low heat, stirring occasionally.

Add the stem ginger to the flour mixture. Whisk the milk mixture into the flour mixture, then whisk in the treacle mixture followed by the egg. When thoroughly blended the mixture should be a thin batter.

Pour the mixture into the prepared tin and bake for 45 minutes to 1 hour or until a skewer inserted into the centre comes out clean. The gingerbread will rise during baking and then fall and shrink slightly as it cools. Leave to cool completely in the tin. Turn out and wrap first in greaseproof paper and then in foil. Keep for a couple of days before slicing.

1 GRATE THE PRESERVED STEM GINGER INTO THE BOWL WITH THE RUBBED-IN MIXTURE.

2 WHISK IN THE SWEETENED MILK AND THEN THE TREACLE AND SYRUP MIXTURE.

Just the way I like it: thick slices of Stem Ginger Gingerbread spread with unsalted butter.

Jim Friedlander loves to experiment and share recipes. Here are his *Apple Almond Cream Pie (see recipe on page 188), Bayberry Bread* and *Granny Glyn's Lemon Loaf.*

BAYBERRY BREAD

Anthony met Jim and Glynrose Friedlander when he stayed at their Federal-style farmhouse in Freeport, Maine. They describe the Isaac Randall House, built in 1823, as a B and B, 'though not as utilitarian as the ones in Britain'. And it is quite out of the ordinary: the kitchen-dining room has a hand-painted floor, an old wood stove (now converted to gas) for cooking, and copper pans and utensils everywhere. The eight bedrooms are furnished with lovely old quilts, oriental rugs, working fireplaces and oil lamps, to give a charming, homely atmosphere.

But the decor is eclipsed by the enormous breakfasts Jim prepares each day. After home-made muesli and fresh fruit salad, he cooks pancakes, french toast (pain perdu), and bacon and eggs to order. To follow there are always a couple of speciality loaves, and even the odd fruit pie (see Apple Almond Cream Pie on page 188).

As Jim says: 'We like to eat, and we like to experiment with recipes we pick up when we travel. Then we like to share them.'

Thank you Jim, and see you soon. Bayberry, by the way, is the local name for cranberry.

INGREDIENTS

Makes 1 medium loaf
140g (5oz) wholemeal bread flour
140g (5oz) plain flour
1¹/₂ teaspoons baking powder
¹/₂ teaspoon bicarbonate of soda
a large pinch of salt
¹/₄ teaspoon ground cinnamon
a large pinch of grated nutmeg
100g (3¹/₂oz) caster sugar
100g (3¹/₂oz) light muscovado sugar
60g (2oz) unsalted butter, chilled and diced
1¹/₂ teaspoons grated orange rind
170ml (6fl oz) freshly squeezed orange juice
1 egg, beaten
110g (4oz) dried cranberries
60g (2oz) pecans or walnuts, roughly chopped
60g (2oz) raisins (optional)

a 450g (1lb) loaf tin or a small roasting tin,
   greased

Preheat the oven to 180C (350F, Gas 4).

Put the flours, baking powder, bicarbonate of soda, salt, spices and sugars into a large mixing bowl and stir until thoroughly combined. Add the diced butter and rub in with your fingertips to make coarse crumbs. Mix the orange rind with the juice and the egg, and add to the dry mixture. Mix briefly, then fold in the cranberries, nuts and raisins. As soon as the mixture is thoroughly blended, spoon it into the prepared tin.

Bake for 1 hour or until golden and firm. A skewer inserted into the centre should come out clean. Turn out on to a wire rack and leave to cool. Serve thickly sliced, with butter. Best when eaten within 3 days.

NOTE To vary the recipe, Jim uses fresh cranberries, blueberries in season, and dried cherries all year round.

GRANNY GLYN'S LEMON LOAF

INGREDIENTS

Makes 1 large loaf
255g (9oz) caster sugar
155g (5¹/₂oz) unsalted butter, at room temperature
3 eggs, beaten
the grated rind of 1¹/₂ unwaxed lemons
280g (10oz) plain flour
¹/₄ teaspoon salt
1¹/₂ teaspoons baking powder
140ml (5fl oz) milk
60g (2oz) ground pecans

TOPPING:
70g (2¹/₂oz) icing sugar, sifted
the juice of 1¹/₂ lemons

a 900g (2lb) loaf tin, greased and lined on the
   bottom

This is another delicious recipe from the Friedlanders of Freeport, Maine. The fresh-tasting lemon loaf cake is easily made by the creaming method. The cake is enriched and flavoured with pecans that have been finely ground in a food processor. To preserve the freshness of the nuts, grind them just before making the cake mixture.

Preheat the oven to 180C (350F, Gas 4).

Put the sugar and butter into a mixing bowl and beat until very light and creamy, using a wooden spoon or electric mixer. Gradually beat in the eggs. Using a large metal spoon, gently stir in the lemon rind. Sift the flour with the salt and baking powder and fold in. Gradually stir in the milk followed by the ground nuts. When the mixture is thoroughly blended, spoon it into the prepared tin.

Bake for about 1 hour or until risen, golden and firm. A cocktail stick inserted into the centre should come out clean.

While the loaf is baking prepare the topping by stirring the icing sugar and lemon juice together until smooth.

Remove the cooked loaf from the oven, and leave it in the tin. Immediately puncture the surface all over with a cocktail stick or skewer and spoon over the topping. Leave to cool completely in the tin. Best eaten within 3 days.

VARIATION Use freshly ground walnuts instead of pecans.

CHAPTER FOUR

FAMILY & CELEBRATION CAKES

From the seemingly plain but luxurious
Quatre-quarts to the richest, most seductive of
chocolate cakes, here are recipes for coffee time
and afternoon tea as well as dessert.

QUATRE-QUARTS OR POUND CAKE

INGREDIENTS

Makes 1 large loaf-shaped cake

4 eggs

about 250g (8³/₄oz) unsalted butter, at room
   temperature

about 250g (8³/₄oz) caster sugar

a pinch of salt

¹/₂ teaspoon pure vanilla essence

about 250g (8³/₄oz) self-raising flour

60g (2oz) crystallised fruit, chopped and soaked in
   2 tablespoons rum overnight

a 900g (2lb) loaf tin, lined with a double thickness
   of greased greaseproof paper

Quatre-quarts was just a rich sponge cake to me until we visited la Maison Bernachon in Lyons. Called the best little chocolate shop in the world, it owes its reputation to father and son perfectionist chocolatiers and pâtissiers, Maurice and Jean-Jacques Bernachon. Beside the divine chocolate, made by hand from scratch, are heavenly cakes and pastries. There is also a salon de thé where you can try in miniature the miracles available in the boutique. Here Jean-Jacques prepared for us a breakfast of coffee and large slices of moist, very rich, angelically light vanilla quatre-quarts studded with fruits confits macerated in rum. Of all their superlative creations this, the simplest, was my favourite. Jean-Jacques showed us the kitchens where trays of freshly picked local fruits were being prepared for the long process of cooking in sugar syrup, which turns them into the luscious fruits confits. A large dish of cherries was being steeped in brandy. The attention to detail is fanatical; there are no short cuts to perfection.

Jean-Jacques explained the intricacies of the seemingly simple quatre-quarts: the eggs must be weighed first and then the same quantity weighed in flour, the finest butter and sugar. The cake can be made in two ways. In the first, the butter is beaten until very creamy; the sugar is gradually beaten in to make a very light and fluffy mixture; the eggs are added a tablespoon at a time while beating vigorously; and, finally, the flour is gently folded in. In the second, the egg yolks and sugar are beaten to a thick foam; the butter is melted and cooled, then folded in, followed by the flour and, finally, the whisked egg whites. This latter method, favoured by the French, makes a lighter, more tender cake, but it tends to be dry, while the former can be heavy and tough if not well made. I tried both ways, following Jean-Jacques' instructions, and preferred the creaming method. Before you begin, be sure that all the ingredients are at room temperature or it will be difficult to incorporate air into the mixture.

Preheat the oven to 200C (400F, Gas 6).

Weigh the 4 eggs together – the total weight should be 250–260g (8³/₄–9¹/₄oz). Use exactly the same weight of butter, sugar and flour.

Put the soft butter in the bowl of an electric mixer and beat at low speed until very creamy. Gradually beat in the sugar, then beat the mixture at high speed until it becomes very white and light in texture. Lightly beat the eggs with the salt, then beat into the creamed mixture a tablespoon at a time, beating well after each addition. This will take at least 7 minutes.

PREVIOUS PAGE Royal Scotsman Fruit Cake
(left), Walnut Cake.

1 BEAT THE BUTTER AND SUGAR TOGETHER
UNTIL VERY WHITE AND LIGHT.

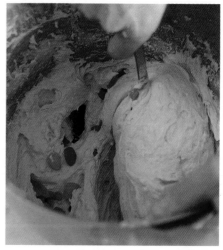

2 ADD THE FLOUR, THEN GENTLY FOLD IN
THE RUM-SOAKED FRUIT.

Quatre-quarts is made with equal weights of eggs, butter, sugar and flour. The recipe here is flavoured with vanilla and includes some luscious rum-soaked crystallised fruit. Alternatively, you can bake a chocolate-flavoured cake and add rum-soaked sultanas.

VARIATION: CHOCOLATE QUATRE-QUARTS Replace 50g (1¾oz) of the weighed flour with the same amount of cocoa and sift into the bowl with the flour and ½ teaspoon baking powder. Use 60g (2oz) sultanas soaked in 2 tablespoons rum instead of the crystallised fruits.

Beat in the vanilla. If the mixture starts to separate or split and slide around in the bowl, add a tablespoon of the flour with the last portions of egg. Sift the flour into the bowl and gently fold into the mixture using a large metal spoon. Try to avoid stirring or beating: cut downwards through the mixture with the edge of the spoon and then fold over; give the bowl a quarter turn and repeat the cutting and folding; continue until there are no more streaks of flour. Add the fruit – it should have absorbed all the rum – and fold it in in the same way.

Spoon the mixture into the prepared tin – it should be three-quarters full. Smooth the surface until level. Bake for 40–50 minutes or until a cocktail stick inserted into the centre comes out clean. Cool in the tin for a minute, then lift the cake out of the tin, peel off the paper and leave to cool completely on a wire rack. Store in an airtight tin, and eat within 5 days. The fruit will tend to settle towards the bottom during cooking, but don't worry – this is quite normal.

SEVILLE ORANGE CAKE

Makes a 20.5cm (8in) round cake
170g (6oz) unsalted butter, at room temperature
170g (6oz) golden caster sugar
3 eggs, size 2, beaten
170g (6oz) self-raising flour
½ teaspoon baking powder
140g (5oz) Seville orange marmalade, gently
  warmed
2 tablespoons milk

ICING:
110g (4oz) icing sugar, sifted
2 tablespoons warm water

a 20.5cm (8in) round deep cake tin, greased and
  lined on the bottom (see pages 112-3)

Dessert oranges often lack sharpness and intense flavour, so it is hard to make a really orangey sponge cake that is not oversweet or cloying. However, good quality Seville orange marmalade, preferably home-made with plenty of chunky peel and a slightly sharp taste, transforms a sponge mixture.

Preheat the oven to 180C (350F, Gas 4).

Beat the butter until creamy, using an electric mixer or wooden spoon. Add the sugar and beat until light and fluffy. Gradually beat in the eggs, beating well after each addition. Sift the flour with the baking powder and gently fold into the mixture using a large metal spoon. When thoroughly blended, add half of the marmalade and the milk and carefully fold in.

Spoon the sponge mixture into the prepared tin and spread to level the surface. Bake in the preheated oven for 45–50 minutes or until golden and firm to the touch. Turn out on to a wire rack and immediately brush with the remaining warm marmalade. Leave to cool completely.

To make the icing, use a wooden spoon to mix the icing sugar and the warm water until smooth and lump-free; the icing should be fairly runny. Spoon over the top of the cake and let it run down the sides. Leave to set — about 1 hour. Store in an airtight tin, and eat within 4 days.

OPPOSITE (from top to bottom) Seville Orange Cake, Cinnamon Apricot Cake, February Cake (see recipe on page 110).

1 BEAT IN THE EGGS LITTLE BY LITTLE.

2 CUT AND FOLD IN THE SIFTED FLOUR.

CINNAMON APRICOT CAKE

Makes a 20.5cm (8in) round cake
130g (4½oz) unsalted butter, at room temperature
130g (4½oz) light muscovado sugar, sifted if
  lumpy
170g (6oz) self-raising flour
1 teaspoon ground cinnamon
30g (1oz) ground almonds
3 eggs, size 2, beaten
140g (5oz) ready-to-eat dried apricots, chopped
20g (¾oz) flaked almonds

a 20.5cm (8in) round deep cake tin, greased and
  lined on the bottom (see pages 112-3)

This lovely moist cake contains plenty of juicy apricots and isn't oversweet.

Preheat the oven to 170C (325F, Gas 3).

Beat the butter until creamy, using a wooden spoon or electric mixer. Add the sugar and beat until light and fluffy. Sift the flour with the cinnamon and ground almonds. Very slowly beat the eggs into the creamed mixture, beating well after each addition and adding a little of the flour mixture with the last batch. Using a metal spoon, carefully fold in the rest of the flour mixture and the apricots. When thoroughly combined, spoon into the prepared tin and level the surface. Sprinkle evenly with the flaked almonds.

Bake in the preheated oven for about 1 hour or until a skewer inserted into the centre comes out clean. Leave to cool in the tin. Store in an airtight tin, and eat within 4 days.

WALNUT CAKE

INGREDIENTS

Makes an 18cm (7in) sandwich cake
170g (6oz) unsalted butter, at room temperature
140g (5oz) golden caster sugar
1 tablespoon golden syrup
2 eggs, size 2, beaten
60g (2oz) walnut pieces, roughly chopped
170g (6oz) self-raising flour, sifted

FILLING:
110g (4oz) unsalted butter, at room temperature
170g (6oz) icing sugar, sifted
a few drops of pure vanilla essence
2 tablespoons hot milk
30g (1oz) walnut pieces, very finely chopped

ICING:
230g (8oz) icing sugar, sifted
2–3 tablespoons hot water
walnut halves for decoration

two 18cm (7in) sandwich tins, greased and lined
   on the bottom (see pages 112-3)

I am very fond of the old-fashioned walnut cakes I remember from childhood, but finding a good recipe has been difficult. The American-style cakes made with oil tasted fine, but the texture seemed too rubbery, while the whisked egg and sugar recipes popular in Europe were too tough and dry. The traditional British method of creaming the butter and sugar then beating in the eggs made a moist but slightly heavy cake. This recipe, with golden syrup, makes a very light but moist and well-flavoured cake that keeps well. The layers of nut sponge are sandwiched with walnut buttercream and then iced with a thick glacé icing.

Preheat the oven to 180C (350F, Gas 4).

Using an electric mixer or a wooden spoon, cream the butter until light, then gradually beat in the sugar. Beat well until the mixture becomes light and fluffy, then beat in the syrup. Gradually beat in the eggs, beating well after each addition. Fold in the walnuts and the sifted flour using a large metal spoon.

Divide the mixture between the prepared tins and smooth the surface. Bake in the preheated oven for 25–30 minutes or until the cakes are springy to the touch. Turn the cakes out of the tins on to a wire rack and leave them to cool.

To make the filling, cream the butter until soft, using an electric mixer or wooden spoon, then beat in the icing sugar at slow speed to make a fluffy smooth mixture. Beat in the vanilla, milk and walnuts.

To make the icing, put the sifted icing sugar into a mixing bowl and work in the hot water using a wooden spoon to make a very smooth, thick, spreadable icing. Cover tightly until ready to use.

To assemble, split each cake in half horizontally using a long sharp knife – the nuts will cause the crumb to tear slightly, so if possible cut the day after baking. Spread a third of the filling on half of one cake then cover with the other piece. Spread with half the remaining filling. Put the base of the second cake on top and spread with the remaining filling. Cover with the last piece of cake. Spread the glacé icing over the top of the cake and ease it down the sides. Use as few movements as possible to avoid a lot of crumbs in the icing. Leave for an hour or so before serving, to allow the icing to set. Store in an airtight tin, and eat within 5 days.

1 WITH THE MACHINE RUNNING, ADD THE GOLDEN SYRUP TO THE MIXTURE.

2 THE CAKES MUST BE COMPLETELY COLD BEFORE YOU SPLIT THEM IN HALF.

This magnificent walnut tree (right), reputed to be one of the largest walnut trees in Britain, is planted in the grounds of Marble Hill House, Twickenham, Surrey (top).

FEBRUARY CAKE

Makes a 20.5cm (8in) round cake

110g (4oz) unsalted butter, at room temperature

85g (3oz) dark muscovado sugar, sifted if lumpy

2 eggs, size 2, beaten

230g (8oz) good mincemeat

1 tablespoon orange juice

170g (6oz) self-raising flour

a little demerara sugar for sprinkling

a 20.5cm (8in) round deep cake tin, greased and
lined on the bottom (see pages 112-3)

I like to save a jar of home-made Christmas mincemeat (see page 137) to make this cake in February. It is usually such a dreary, wet month, and a good cake cheers us all up. This is a very quick and simple cake to make and has all the rich spicy flavours of the well-matured mincemeat.

Preheat the oven to 170C (325F, Gas 3).

Using an electric mixer or wooden spoon, beat the butter until creamy. Add the sugar and beat until light and fluffy. Gradually beat in the eggs, beating well after each addition. Stir in the mincemeat, orange juice and flour using a large metal spoon. When thoroughly blended, spoon the mixture into the prepared tin and level the surface. Sprinkle evenly with a little demerara sugar.

Bake in the preheated oven for 1–1¼ hours or until a skewer inserted into the centre comes out clean. The cake will have slight cracks. Loosen the cake and turn it out on to a wire rack to cool completely. Wrap in greaseproof paper, put into an airtight tin and keep for a day before cutting. Eat within a week.

1 *AFTER THE EGGS HAVE BEEN MIXED IN, ADD THE RICH, MOIST MINCEMEAT.*

2 *ADD THE ORANGE JUICE FOLLOWED BY THE FLOUR AND COMBINE THOROUGHLY.*

3 *THE MIXTURE WILL BE QUITE STIFF. SPOON IT INTO THE CAKE TIN.*

4 *SMOOTH THE SURFACE, THEN SPRINKLE WITH SOME DEMERARA SUGAR.*

ROYAL SCOTSMAN FRUIT CAKE

INGREDIENTS

Makes a 20.5cm (8in) round cake

230g (8oz) plain flour

1½ teaspoons baking powder

a pinch of salt

170g (6oz) unsalted butter, at room temperature

170g (6oz) light muscovado sugar

4 eggs, beaten

60g (2oz) ground almonds

340g (12oz) mixed dried fruit and chopped candied peel

110g (4oz) naturally coloured glacé cherries, rinsed, dried and halved

1–2 tablespoons milk

230g (8oz) white marzipan

45g (1½oz) flaked almonds

a 20.5cm (8in) round deep cake tin, greased and lined with greased greaseproof paper (see pages 112-3)

ABOVE RIGHT Glen Nevis, Fort William, Scotland.

The baked Royal Scotsman Fruit Cake, straight from the oven.

Years ago I was lucky enough to have a very short trip on the famous steam train, the Royal Scotsman. Travelling around Scotland on this train is true luxury — enjoying the glorious scenery of God's Own Country in wonderful comfort and with excellent Scottish food. This rich, moist fruit cake, with its hidden layer of marzipan, was served at tea with pistachio shortbreads. It has become a firm favourite with my family.

Preheat the oven to 180C (350F, Gas 4).

Sift the flour with the baking powder and salt, and set aside. Using an electric mixer, beat the butter until creamy, then gradually beat in the sugar. Beat until very light and fluffy. Gradually beat in the eggs, beating well after each addition. Add a tablespoon of the flour with the last two additions of egg. Using a large metal spoon, fold in the rest of the flour and the ground almonds. When thoroughly blended, fold in the fruit mixture and the cherries. Add enough milk to make a mixture that just falls from the spoon when tapped.

Spoon half the mixture into the prepared tin and smooth the surface. Roll out the marzipan into a disc to fit the tin and place it gently on top of the cake mixture. Spoon the rest of the mixture on top. Smooth the surface, then make a slight hollow in the centre so the cake will rise evenly. Sprinkle with the flaked almonds.

Bake in the preheated oven for 30 minutes, then reduce the oven temperature to 170C (325F, Gas 3) and bake for a further 1¼–1½ hours or until a skewer inserted into the centre of the cake, just down to the marzipan layer, comes out clean. (The marzipan will be soft and sticky, so if you push the skewer into it it will be hard to tell if the cake itself is cooked.) Leave to cool completely in the tin before turning out. Remove the greaseproof paper, then wrap in clean paper and keep in an airtight tin for about 3 days before cutting.

KATIE STEWART'S DUNDEE CAKE

INGREDIENTS

Makes a 20.5cm (8in) round cake

170g (6oz) plain flour

110g (4oz) self-raising flour

1/2 teaspoon salt

60g (2oz) ground almonds

170g (6oz) butter, at room temperature

60g (2oz) white vegetable fat, at room temperature

230g (8oz) light muscovado sugar, sifted if lumpy

4 eggs, size 2, at room temperature

the finely grated rind of 1 unwaxed lemon

340g (12oz) sultanas

230g (8oz) currants

110g (4oz) chopped mixed candied peel

about 18 blanched almond halves

a 20.5cm (8in) round deep cake tin, greased and
    lined with greased greaseproof paper (see below)
a baking tray and plenty of newspaper

1 KATIE ALWAYS USES HER HAND TO
CREAM THE FAT WITH THE SUGAR.

2 SHE WRAPS THICK NEWSPAPER AROUND
THE TIN TO PREVENT SCORCHING.

The Scots have a long tradition of baking, and Dundee has a reputation for the richest, most luxurious fruit cakes. Spices, sugar, and citrus and dried fruits arrived at the port from overseas, and fine white wheat flour was imported from England. This cake dates from the 17th century when it was a favourite at the court of Mary Queen of Scots — the royal bakers indulged the Queen's sweet tooth, her love of ostentation and her dislike of cherries with a cake that was packed with expensive and uncommon ingredients.

Katie Stewart has long been a heroine of mine, ever since I spent a school holiday cooking every single recipe in her Times Cookery Book. Katie, who comes from Aberdeen, has had an illustrious career. Like her mother she trained at the Domestic Science School in Aberdeen before moving down to London and Westminster College. After even more training — at the Cordon Bleu in Paris — Katie worked as a home economist for Nestlé in White Plains, New York. She started writing for Woman's Mirror in 1959, then moved on to The Times and Woman's Journal, where she has been Cookery Editor for 26 years.

Katie's fruit cakes, baked to recipes handed down from her mother, are superb, and it was a great treat to watch her make them at her house in Sussex.

Preheat the oven to 180C (350F, Gas 4).

Sift the flours with the salt and almonds, and set aside.

In a large mixing bowl cream the fats and sugar together until soft and light, using your hand, a wooden spoon or an electric mixer. Katie uses her hand for this — she says it is messy but quick. Mix the eggs with the grated lemon rind. Beat the egg mixture into the creamed mixture a little at a time — at least five batches — beating well after each addition. If the mixture starts to curdle or slide around in the bowl, add some of the sifted flour mixture with the last few additions of the egg mixture. Mix a tablespoon of the flour with the fruit and peel. Using a metal spoon, lightly fold half of the remaining flour into the creamed mixture, then add the fruit mixture and, finally, the rest of the flour. Gently mix to make a medium soft consistency: the mixture should drop off the spoon when it is given a gentle shake.

Spoon the mixture into the prepared tin and spread level with a spoon, gently pressing the mixture down. Lightly moisten the top of the cake with wet knuckles; this will prevent a hard dry crust from forming before the cake has set. Place the almond halves on top in a neat circle. Tie newspaper, folded into four thicknesses, around the tin to prevent scorched or dry sides. Put a tray of water on the floor of the oven — this helps to keep the cake moist.

Set the cake tin on a thick pad of newspaper on a baking tray and bake in the centre of the preheated oven for 45 minutes. Lower the oven temperature to 170C (325F, Gas 3) and bake for a further 1 3/4 hours — giving a total cooking time of 2 1/2 hours. Leave the cake to cool in the tin overnight before turning out. When the cake is quite cold — 24 hours after baking — wrap it in greaseproof paper and store in an airtight tin for a week before cutting.

LINING A ROUND CAKE TIN

Many cakes need only to have the bottom of the tin lined, but when baking a fruit-rich cake, all tins — even non-stick ones — should be lined on the

Katie in her kitchen with Charlie, the dog. On the table are freshly baked Queen Mary Tartlets (see recipe on page 140) and Dundee Cake.

bottom and around the sides, using heavy greaseproof paper or non-stick baking parchment. The lining prevents the cake from sticking to the tin. For fruit cakes with a long baking period, the lining on the bottom and sides also helps prevent the cake from scorching and drying out.

First, brush the inside of the tin with melted butter so the paper will adhere – for good smooth sides it is important the paper does not become wrinkled. Cut out a disc of greaseproof paper to fit the bottom of the tin: set the tin on a sheet of paper and draw around the base. If only lining the bottom of the tin, put the disc of paper in place. If lining the sides as well, first measure the circumference and depth of the tin; cut a strip of paper the same length as the circumference and three times as wide as the depth of the tin. Fold the paper strip in half lengthways. Turn up the folded edge 2.5cm (1in) and snip this, up to the turned-up fold, at 2.5cm (1in) intervals. Brush the paper above the snipped edge with melted butter, then fit the paper strip inside the tin so the snipped edge lies flat on the bottom and the rest smoothly lines the side. Put the disc into the tin to cover the bottom and the snipped paper edge.

Gâteau Noir (left) and Stout Cake.

STOUT CAKE

INGREDIENTS

Makes a 20.5cm (8in) round cake

170g (6oz) best quality large seedless raisins

170g (6oz) best quality sultanas

7 tablespoons stout

170g (6oz) unsalted butter, at room temperature

170g (6oz) dark muscovado sugar, sifted

3 eggs, beaten

230g (8oz) plain flour

1½ teaspoons ground mixed spice

60g (2oz) chopped mixed candied peel

85g (3oz) walnut pieces

a 20.5cm (8in) round deep cake tin, greased and
lined with greased greaseproof paper (see
pages 112-3)

This is a dark, spiced fruit cake made with sultanas and raisins soaked in stout, plus walnuts for extra crunch. Made with the best fruit, it will be a good keeper, and can be covered with marzipan and white icing – royal or ready-to-roll.

Put the raisins and sultanas in a bowl and pour over the stout. Mix well, then cover tightly and leave to soak overnight.

Next day, preheat the oven to 170C (325F, Gas 3).

Beat the butter until light, using an electric mixer or wooden spoon. Gradually beat in the sifted sugar, then continue beating until the mixture becomes lighter and fluffy in texture. Gradually beat in the eggs, beating well after each addition. Sift the flour and the mixed spice into the bowl, and carefully fold in using a large metal spoon. Add the soaked fruit and any liquid left in the bowl, followed by the mixed peel and the walnuts. When thoroughly blended, spoon into the prepared tin and smooth the surface level.

Bake in the preheated oven for 1½ hours or until a skewer inserted into the centre comes out clean. If the top of the cake looks as if it is becoming too brown, cover with a double sheet of greaseproof paper. Leave to cool in the tin, then turn out. Remove the lining paper and wrap in fresh greaseproof paper. Store in an airtight tin for 3–5 days before cutting.

GÂTEAU NOIR

Makes 1 very large cake

140ml (5fl oz) each rum, port, brandy, cherry brandy and water

2 teaspoons Angostura bitters

1 teaspoon ground cinnamon

1 cinnamon stick

1 teaspoon freshly grated nutmeg

½ teaspoon ground cloves

½ teaspoon ground allspice

½ teaspoon salt

2 tablespoons molasses sugar

2kg (about 4lb 6oz) mixed dried and candied fruit and peel

450g (1lb) unsalted butter, at room temperature

450g (1lb) demerara sugar

8 eggs, size 2, beaten

450g (1lb) self-raising flour, sifted

110g (4oz) chopped mixed nuts – pecans and almonds for choice

2 teaspoons pure vanilla essence

a roasting tin, about 29 x 34cm (11½ x 13½in), lined with greased foil

The legendary Creole Christmas cake, heavy – in every sense – with dried fruits and liquor, is not for the faint-hearted. It is very rich, and moist enough to be eaten as a pudding. I enjoy it with strong coffee. The recipe calls for a lot of ingredients, but the method is simple. I use the 'luxury fruit' mixture available in 500g packets at my local supermarket, although you can use your own mixture of raisins, sultanas, currants, mixed candied peel, chopped dried apricots and prunes, glacé pineapple and cherries. The fruits are simmered with the spices and alcohols to plump them up. Then, after a few days of soaking, they are mixed with the rest of the ingredients and baked in a large roasting tin. Once you have tried this cake you may never go back to the traditional British Christmas cake – I haven't.

Put the rum, port, brandy, cherry brandy, water, bitters, ground and stick cinnamon, nutmeg, cloves, allspice, salt, molasses sugar and the fruit mixture into a large non-aluminium saucepan. Bring slowly to the boil, then simmer gently for 10 minutes, stirring frequently. The mixture will be moist, but most of the liquid will have been absorbed. Tip into a large heatproof glass or china bowl and leave to cool completely. Then cover and leave for 3–5 days to mature, stirring every day.

When ready to bake the cake, preheat the oven to 140C (275F, Gas 1).

Put the butter into a very large mixing bowl with the demerara sugar and beat until fairly light, using a wooden spoon. Gradually beat in the eggs – this is quite hard work but the mixture does not need to beaten as thoroughly as a sponge cake (see Quatre-quarts, page 104). Some of the flour can be added with the last few portions of egg to prevent the mixture from curdling or splitting. Stir in the rest of the flour using a large metal spoon, then work in the fruit mixture, with any liquid left in the bowl, the nuts and the vanilla essence. When thoroughly blended, spoon into the prepared tin and level the surface.

Cover the tin quite loosely with a double layer of greaseproof paper, then bake for about 3½ hours or until just cooked in the centre; test with a skewer – the cake should be quite moist. Leave to cool completely in the tin, then turn out and peel off the foil. Wrap in greaseproof paper and store in an airtight container for several days before cutting.

1 AFTER 3–5 DAYS OF MARINATING IN LIQUOR AND SPICES, THE FRUIT MIXTURE IS VERY MOIST AND SOFT.

2 WHEN WELL MIXED, SPOON THE HEAVY, FRUIT-DENSE CAKE MIXTURE INTO THE FOIL-LINED ROASTING TIN.

RHUBARB CHEESECAKE

INGREDIENTS

Makes a 25.5–28cm (10–11in) cake, to
    serve 10–12
CRUST:
110g (4oz) digestive biscuits, crushed
1/2 teaspoon ground ginger
30g (1oz) caster sugar
60g (2oz) unsalted butter, melted

FILLING:
900g (2lb) cream cheese
the grated rind of 1 unwaxed lemon
1 teaspoon pure vanilla essence
200g (7oz) caster sugar
4 eggs, size 2, beaten
455ml (16fl oz) soured cream

TOPPING:
250g (8³/₄oz) trimmed young rhubarb, rinsed
3 tablespoons redcurrant or seedless raspberry jelly

a 25.5–28cm (10-11in) springclip tin, greased
a baking tray

My ideal cheesecake is deep and rich, yet light and fluffy, with plenty of flavour. My husband, who is from New York, likes the heavy middle-European kind of cheesecake that sticks briefly to the top of your mouth and then lingers around the hips. Both types are baked rather than set with gelatine, and can be left plain or topped with fresh or poached fruit and then a glaze. This recipe is my favourite – sorry Alan – and is covered with the tender young forced rhubarb available in the spring. As this delicate fruit breaks up very readily, it is cooked slowly in the oven in redcurrant or raspberry jelly and the juices are used for the glaze. Other fruit toppings could be raspberries or strawberries, poached or fresh apricots or peaches, the large dessert blackberries of the Fantasia variety, mixed currants, figs or cherries. As a glaze choose a jelly or sieved jam to suit the fruit. For some reason the Philadelphia brand of cream cheese works best in this recipe – I have had disappointing results with other cream cheeses.

Preheat the oven to 300F (150C, Gas 2).

To make the crust, mix the biscuit crumbs with the ground ginger, sugar and melted butter. Tip the mixture into the prepared tin, then press on to the bottom, using the back of a spoon, to make an even layer. Chill for 30 minutes while making the filling.

Put the cream cheese, grated lemon rind, vanilla and sugar into the bowl of an electric mixer (the mixture can also be beaten by hand using a wooden spoon, but it is hard work). Beat at low speed until the mixture is very smooth, then increase the speed and gradually beat in the eggs, scraping down the sides of the bowl from time to time. When well mixed, pour in the soured cream and stir with a wooden spoon until the mixture is thoroughly combined.

1 PRESS THE CRUMB MIXTURE FIRMLY INTO THE BOTTOM OF THE SPRINGCLIP TIN.

2 THOROUGHLY WASH THE LEMON, THEN GRATE THE RIND INTO THE BOWL.

3 WHEN THE CHEESE AND CREAM MIXTURE IS SMOOTH, POUR IT INTO THE TIN.

4 CUT THE RHUBARB NEATLY, THEN COOK IN A BAKING DISH WITH THE JELLY.

BRUSH THE RHUBARB WITH THE HOT SYRUPY COOKING JUICES TO GLAZE.

Pour the filling into the tin – it should be seven-eighths full – and set the tin on a baking tray. Bake in the preheated oven for 1¾–2 hours or until just firm. The cheesecake will puff up, but it will sink on cooling and then usually cracks across the middle.

When the cheesecake is cooked, turn off the oven and open the door a few inches – wedge it if necessary. Leave the cheesecake inside to cool slowly for 1 hour. Then remove from the oven, set the tin on a wire rack and leave until completely cold. Cover and chill overnight before turning out and decorating.

To make the topping, preheat the oven to 180C (350F, Gas 4). Cut the rhubarb into pieces about 3cm (1¼in) long. Spread the jelly on the bottom of a baking dish and arrange the rhubarb in a single layer on top. Cover and cook in the preheated oven for about 20 minutes or until just tender, stirring very gently from time to time. Leave to cool.

When ready to decorate the cheesecake, remove the rhubarb from the liquid, draining well. Spoon the rhubarb cooking juices into a small pan and bring to the boil. Simmer until syrupy. Arrange the fruit on top of the unmoulded cheesecake, then brush with the hot syrup. Chill until set – about 30 minutes – before serving. Store in a covered container in the fridge, and eat within 3 days.

CHOCOLATE, THE FOOD OF THE GODS

RIGHT *Sacks of cocoa beans waiting to be mixed and roasted at the Bernachon maison du chocolat in Lyons.*

BELOW *After roasting for 20 minutes the cocoa beans have to be cooled before shelling.*

BOTTOM *Noël Sevre can tell whether or not the beans have been properly roasted by their smell.*

Until I went to Lyons, the nearest I had come to the principal ingredient of chocolate was the *Theobroma cacao* in the Princess of Wales Conservatory in Kew Gardens. This 'food of the gods' tree, which grows to almost 20 metres in the wild and around 4 metres on plantations, is found in tropical America and Africa. The large yellow-green fruits of the tree contain white juicy pulp and hard bitter seeds, and it is these seeds from which chocolate and cocoa are made.

After the fruits are harvested and the seeds removed, they are left to ferment for 4–6 days – the heat of this fermentation kills the seed's embryo and starts chemical reactions that change the initial inedibly bitter taste. Next, the seeds – now beans – are dried in the sun, and then they are put into sacks for sale.

It was a hot, sticky day when I visited the Bernachon *maison du chocolat* in Lyons. I expected to be greeted by a cloying smell which would put me off all sweets for weeks. Instead there was merely a slightly heady, bitter aroma. The factory is, in fact, a chocolate-making *atelier* – one room containing all that is required. In one corner the ingredients are neatly arranged: sacks of beans, bags of crystal sugar, a shoe box of glossy vanilla pods and a bowl of melted cocoa butter.

Unlike coffee, chocolate cannot be made with just one type of bean, and it is the blend of beans – up to 12 varieties here – that gives the final product its special flavour. Jean-Jacques Bernachon only buys the finest and most costly beans: chuao from Venezuela, para from Brazil, the santa-fe, sambirand and guayaquil from Trinidad and Ecuador. He compares the beans to the premiers grands crus wines of Bordeaux – each variety has an individual character and adds a different quality to the blend: aroma, bitterness, depth of flavour or richness.

The chocolate-maker, Noël Sevre, explained the process chez Bernachon. The almond-shaped beans are first picked over by hand to check for damage: each variety is a different colour, ranging from pale coffee to a rich mahogany brown. They are then roasted – like coffee – for

ABOVE *After a day and a half of conchage, the finished chocolate is poured into trays and left to set into blocks.*

RIGHT *Jean-Jacques Bernachon and his pride and joy – the gâteau president.*

20 minutes at 180C, which cracks the shells and releases a pleasant toasty smell. Once cooled the beans are lightly crushed to remove the shells without damaging the precious kernels. These are then ground to make a paste, and are mixed in small batches with melted cocoa butter from Holland, a little sugar – the quantity depends on how the chocolate will be used – and real vanilla from Madagascar. The resulting dryish, clay-like 'dough' is mixed and put through a giant mangle three times, a process called *broyage*. The final key step is *conchage*, or conching, a long slow operation – around 36 hours here – which gently melts and stirs or grinds the ingredients until smooth and mellow. The resulting chocolate is then set as blocks.

ABOVE Hand-made chocolates are given the gold-leaf treatment before they are dispatched to Paul Bocuse's restaurant.

BELOW Maison Bernachon sells incomparable pâtisserie and gâteaux, as well as the famous chocolates. If you cannot wait until you reach home, you can taste everything in the tea shop/restaurant next door.

Cocoa beans contain roughly 50% fat and 50% meat or solids. Pressing the cocoa paste releases some of the fat from the ground kernels – this is the cocoa butter. If the pressed paste is then further ground up and dried it becomes cocoa powder. Cocoa butter is added to the chocolate mixture to increase the fat content, to make it smoother, and to make it melt in the mouth as it has a low melting point. The quantity of cocoa solids – the dry cocoa paste plus the added cocoa butter – determines the quality and depth of flavour of the chocolate. *Couverture*, used for fillings and icings, is around 55%; *amer* or bitter is 65%; *super amer* or extra bitter (best for eating and making desserts and fine cakes) is around 70%; and *sans sucre* or unsweetened (used for sauces by the catering trade) is 100%. Always avoid chocolate labelled as 'cooking' because it may contain just 30% solids.

Great care must be taken when melting chocolate because if it is overheated it easily scorches and becomes a hard solid mass. The best way to melt it is to put the chopped chocolate into a heatproof basin set over a pan of hot but not boiling water. The water should not touch the base of the bowl, nor should the chocolate come into contact with steam from the water. Stir gently until smooth, then remove the bowl from the heat.

Sadly, the production of chocolate at Maison Bernachon is small, and Jean-Jacques will not allow it to be sold anywhere else. So a trip to Lyons or a visit to Paul Bocuse's restaurant nearby is the only way to taste chocolate perfection. Jean-Jacques is married to the great chef's daughter, Jeanne, who runs the Bernachon Passion tea shop/restaurant. Bocuse serves their hand-made chocolates, flecked with real gold leaf, and the *president gâteau*, created by Maurice, Jean-Jacques' father. This triumph of the chocolatier and the pâtissier resembles one of the Queen Mother's Ascot hats with its ruffles and frills, except that she never wears brown.

DEVIL'S FOOD CAKE

INGREDIENTS

Makes a 20.5cm (8in) sandwich cake
85g (3oz) good dark chocolate, chopped
110g (4oz) unsalted butter
85g (3oz) dark muscovado sugar
1 tablespoon golden syrup
170g (6oz) plain flour
30g (1oz) cocoa powder
1/2 teaspoon bicarbonate of soda
2 eggs, size 2, beaten
6 tablespoons milk

FILLING AND ICING:
40g (1¹/₂oz) unsalted butter, at room temperature
40g (1¹/₂oz) cocoa powder
280g (10oz) icing sugar
6 tablespoons milk
2 teaspoons strong black coffee

two 18cm (7in) sandwich tins, greased and lined
   on the bottom (see pages 112-3)

*Above right SPREAD THE SOFT ICING
THICKLY OVER THE ASSEMBLED CAKE, THEN
LEAVE OVERNIGHT BEFORE CUTTING.*

It has taken me a long time to find a really good recipe for this popular cake. Most devil's food cakes look impressive but taste of little except sugar. This unorthodox recipe makes a light cake that is not too deep but has plenty of flavour. The rich chocolate fudge icing contrasts well with the slightly bitter double chocolate sponge. Like most chocolate cakes it is best left overnight before cutting.

Preheat the oven to 170C (325F, Gas 3).
   To make the cake, put the chocolate, butter, sugar and golden syrup in a saucepan set over low heat and melt, stirring frequently. Remove from the heat and leave to cool.
   Sift the flour, cocoa and bicarbonate of soda into a mixing bowl. Make a well in the centre and pour in the cooled melted chocolate mixture. Stir with the flour until well mixed, then add the eggs and milk and beat gently until the mixture is thoroughly combined.
   Spoon the mixture into the prepared tins and spread evenly. Bake for 20–25 minutes or until firm to the touch. Leave to cool completely before turning out of the tins.
   To make the filling and icing mixture, beat the butter until creamy, using a wooden spoon or electric mixer. Sift the cocoa and icing sugar into the bowl, and add the milk and coffee. Mix on low speed until combined, then beat vigorously until smooth and creamy. Taste and add a little more cocoa or coffee if necessary.
   Spread a third of this mixture on one of the cakes and set the second cake on top. Spread the rest of the mixture evenly over the top and down the sides. Cover and leave in a cool place – but not the fridge – overnight so that the icing can become firm and the cake can mature. The cake is best eaten within 3 days.

PECAN FUDGE CAKE

INGREDIENTS

Makes a 22cm (8¾in) round cake
340g (12oz) good dark chocolate
170g (6oz) unsalted butter
60g (2oz) cocoa powder, sifted
5 eggs, size 2
255g (9oz) caster sugar
100g (3½oz) pecans, roughly chopped
icing sugar for dusting

a 22cm (8¾in) springclip tin, greased and lined
on the bottom (see pages 112-3)

This is a wonderfully rich and moist cake, more like a heavy mousse than a sponge because it contains no flour. The rich but not sweet taste comes from a combination of dark chocolate (which must contain at least 70% cocoa solids) and cocoa powder. It can be served as a dessert with vanilla ice-cream or crème anglaise (see page 58).

Preheat the oven to 180C (350F, Gas 4).

Put the chocolate and butter in a heavy saucepan, or in a heatproof bowl set over a pan of hot but not boiling water, and melt very gently, stirring frequently. Remove from the heat and stir in the cocoa. Leave to

1 WHISK THE EGGS WITH THE SUGAR UNTIL THE MIXTURE IS THICK ENOUGH TO MAKE A RIBBON-LIKE TRAIL.

2 REMOVE THE BOWL FROM THE HEAT AND GENTLY FOLD IN THE COOL CHOCOLATE MIXTURE WITH A LARGE SPOON.

3 FINALLY, MIX IN THE CHOPPED PECANS. SPOON INTO THE PREPARED CAKE TIN AND BAKE IMMEDIATELY.

cool while whisking the eggs: put the eggs into a large heatproof bowl and whisk briefly. Add the sugar and set the bowl over a pan of simmering water; the water should not touch the base of the bowl. Whisk, using an electric hand mixer, until the mixture is very light and fluffy and has tripled in bulk. When the whisk is lifted out of the mixture it should leave a very visible ribbon-like trail on the surface. Remove the bowl from the heat and carefully fold in the chocolate mixture, followed by the pecans. Spoon into the prepared tin and smooth the the surface.

Bake for 35 minutes. The top of the cake will be firm but the inside should still be moist – if this cake is overcooked it will be too dry and crumbly to slice. Leave to cool completely in the tin, then turn out and dust with sifted icing sugar. Store in an airtight tin, and eat within 4 days.

BELOW Devil's Food Cake (see recipe on page 121), Pecan Fudge Cake.

THE BEST CHOCOLATE CAKE

INGREDIENTS

Makes 1 heart-shaped cake
110g (4oz) good dark chocolate, chopped
110g (4oz) unsalted butter, at room temperature
85g (3oz) caster sugar
4 eggs, size 2, separated
110g (4oz) ground almonds
a pinch of salt

GANACHE ICING:
115 ml (4fl oz) double cream
110g (4oz) good dark chocolate, chopped

a heart-shaped tin, 21cm (8¹/₄in) long from tip
and 20cm (about 7³/₄in) across the centre,
greased and lined on the bottom

I have yet to find a cake to better this one. It is rich and very chocolatey but not sweet or cloying; it is moist but not heavy. But however carefully it is prepared it will only be as good as the chocolate used. Top quality dark chocolate with over 70% cocoa solids contains less sugar than poor quality or cooking chocolate, which usually has flavourings and other additives as well.

The recipe originally came from Jean-Pierre St Martin, the chef-patron of the Viscos restaurant in the tiny village of St Savin, perched high up in the Pyrenees in south-west France. For his cake, he used 8 large eggs and 250g of everything else — butter, sugar, chocolate and ground almonds — but gradually, through experimentation, I have reduced the sugar. There is no flour in the recipe, nor any raising agent — the lightness comes from the whisked egg whites. The cake is covered with a ganache made from equal quantities of chocolate and cream. For a softer, more fudgy icing use a little more cream than chocolate; for a harder, darker and more intense coating use a little more chocolate than cream.

Although I suggest a heart-shaped tin, you can also use a 20.5cm (8in) round cake tin. Double quantity cake mixture will fit a 24cm (9¹/₂in) round cake tin — ideal for a birthday cake.

Preheat the oven to 200C (400F, Gas 6).

Very gently melt the chocolate in a heatproof bowl set over a pan of hot but not boiling water. Stir until smooth, then remove from the heat and leave to cool while preparing the rest of the mixture. Using an electric mixer or wooden spoon, cream the butter until light in a mixing bowl.

Add the sugar and beat until fluffy, then beat in the egg yolks one at a time, beating well after each addition. Beat in the cooled chocolate, then stir in the almonds using a large metal spoon.

In a spotlessly clean, grease-free bowl, whisk the egg whites with the pinch of salt until they form soft peaks. Gently fold them into the chocolate mixture in three batches using a large metal spoon.

Spoon into the prepared tin and level the surface. Bake in the preheated oven for 15 minutes, then reduce the oven temperature to 180C (350F, Gas 4) and bake for about 10 minutes longer or until just cooked in the centre (test with a skewer). It is important not to overcook this cake or it will not be moist. Run a round-bladed knife around the side of the tin to loosen the cake, but do not turn it out. Set the tin on a wet tea towel and leave to cool. When cold turn out the cake, wrap in greaseproof paper and store in an airtight tin to mature for a day before icing.

To make the ganache icing, heat the cream until scalding hot but not boiling. Remove from the heat and add the chopped chocolate. Leave until completely melted and smooth, stirring occasionally. When cool and thick enough to spread, use to cover the sides and top of the cake. Leave to set in a cool spot – not the fridge (chilling will make the cake hard and the icing will have beads of condensation when it is served). Eat within 4 days.

Jean-Pierre St Martin outside his restaurant, Les Viscos, in south-west France.

1 BE SURE THE MELTED CHOCOLATE IS COMPLETELY COOLED BEFORE BEATING IT INTO THE CAKE MIXTURE.

2 ONCE THE CHOCOLATE HAS BEEN INCORPORATED, USE A LARGE SPOON TO FOLD IN THE GROUND ALMONDS.

3 IN A SPOTLESSLY CLEAN BOWL, USING CLEAN BEATERS, WHISK THE EGG WHITES JUST UNTIL SOFT PEAKS FORM.

4 TO KEEP ALL THE AIR THAT HAS BEEN WHISKED IN, FOLD THE WHITES INTO THE MIXTURE IN THREE BATCHES.

HAZELNUT MERINGUE GÂTEAU

INGREDIENTS

Makes a 20.5cm (8in) gâteau, to serve
    8–10

CAKE:

185g (6¹/₂oz) skinned hazelnuts
185g (6¹/₂oz) caster sugar
6 egg whites, size 2
a pinch of salt

FILLING AND ICING:

500ml (about 18fl oz) double cream
350g (about 12¹/₂oz) good dark chocolate, chopped
cocoa powder for sprinkling

2 baking trays, lined with non-stick baking
    parchment (see recipe)
a piping bag fitted with a 2cm (³/₄in) plain tube

This is a slightly simplifed version of one of Maison Bernachon's most famous gâteaux. It is not very difficult to make, yet tastes wonderful and looks very French and glamorous. The cake part is made from a meringue flavoured with toasted and ground hazelnuts, and the filling and icing are a thick ganache of double cream and dark rich chocolate. (Be sure to use chocolate with at least 70% cocoa solids.) The assembled gâteau should be chilled overnight before cutting.

Preheat the oven to 170C (325F, Gas 3).

Draw a 20.5cm (8in) circle on two sheets of non-stick baking parchment. Use to line the baking trays, turning the paper over so the drawn circle is on the underside.

Put the hazelnuts into a roasting tin or baking dish and toast in the preheated oven until a good even brown. Cool, then work in a food processor to make a coarse powder. Mix the hazelnuts with 170g (6oz) of the sugar and set aside.

Put the egg whites and pinch of salt into a spotlessly clean, grease-free, non-plastic bowl – a stainless steel mixer bowl is fine. Whisk the whites, starting slowly and then gradually increasing the speed, until soft peaks form. Whisk in the remaining 15g (¹/₂oz) sugar at high speed, then continue whisking until the whites form stiff peaks. Using a large metal spoon, gently fold in the hazelnut and sugar mixture.

1 GENTLY COMBINE THE POWDERED
HAZELNUT MIXTURE AND THE MERINGUE.

2 PIPE THE HAZELNUT MERINGUE MIXTURE
IN A SPIRAL TO MAKE A NEAT DISC.

Spoon half the meringue mixture into the piping bag fitted with the plain tube. Pipe on to one of the baking trays in a disc inside the drawn circle: start at the centre and pipe round and round in circles outwards. Use the remaining mixture to pipe a second disc in the same way. Bake the discs in the preheated oven for 1–1¹/₂ hours or until golden, firm and crisp, turning and rotating the trays so the discs cook evenly. Leave to cool completely, then peel off the paper.

Meanwhile, prepare the chocolate filling. Heat the cream in a heavy saucepan until scalding hot but not boiling. Remove from the heat and gradually stir in the chocolate. Stir gently until completely melted and smooth, then leave to cool, stirring occasionally, until the mixture is thick enough to spread. You can hasten the process by chilling the cooled mixture. If it becomes too cold and hard to spread, warm it gently.

To assemble the gâteau, put one disc of hazelnut meringue on to a serving platter and spread with about a third of the chocolate cream mixture, using a palette knife. Put the second meringue disc on top. Quickly spread the rest of the chocolate mixture over the top and down the sides to cover completely. It does not matter if the icing is not completely smooth. If the chocolate becomes hard to spread it may help to dip the palette knife in hot water. Wipe the excess chocolate mixture off the plate, then chill the gâteau overnight.

Remove from the fridge about 30 minutes before serving, unless the weather is very hot, and dust liberally with cocoa powder. Keep in the fridge in a covered container, and eat within 2 days.

A SIMPLE WEDDING CAKE

Makes a 25.5cm (10in) round cake
450g (1lb) unsalted butter, at room temperature
the finely grated rind and juice of 3 large unwaxed
 lemons
450g (1lb) caster sugar
8 eggs, beaten
170g (6oz) ground almonds
230g (8oz) self-raising flour
40g (1^1/$_2$oz) cornflour
^{3}/$_4$ teaspoon baking powder
2–3 tablespoons milk, if necessary

TO COVER WITH MARZIPAN:
about 5 tablespoons lemon curd (see recipe opposite)
icing sugar for dusting
900g (2lb) marzipan

TO COVER WITH SUGAR PASTE ICING:
a little sherry or brandy for brushing
1.1 kg (2^1/$_2$lb) ready-to-roll sugar paste icing

a 25.5cm (10in) round deep cake tin, greased and
 lined with greased greaseproof paper (see
 pages 112-3)
a large round cake board, about 33cm (13in) in
 diameter
flowers to decorate

1 MAKE A SOFT DROPPING CONSISTENCY.

2 TEST THE CAKE WITH A FINE SKEWER.

I like this cake so much I made it for my own wedding two years ago. It is a lovely rich sponge, flavoured with ground almonds and lemon, and is fairly quick and simple to make. Even though I covered the cake with marzipan and white icing like a traditional bride cake, I was anticipating a few raised eye-brows. However, most guests asked for a second piece — and the recipe. I made the cake on the Wednesday before my Saturday wedding, and it took only about two hours from start to finish. The next day I covered it in marzipan, ready made, and left it to dry for 24 hours before covering in ready-to-roll sugar paste icing. Just before the wedding party, I decorated the top and the base of the cake with roses and flowering herbs to match my bouquet.

A half quantity of the cake mixture can be baked in a 21.5cm (8^1/$_2$in) tin, then covered with 800g (1^3/$_4$lb) marzipan and 900g (2lb) icing. Because of the long baking time it is important to prepare the tin well — use three layers of greaseproof or baking parchment for lining, and cover the cake during baking if necessary.

Preheat the oven to 180C (350F, Gas 4).

Beat the butter with the lemon rind until soft and creamy, using an electric mixer. Gradually beat in the sugar, then beat until the mixture becomes very pale and fluffy. Beat in the eggs a tablespoon at a time, beating well after each addition. Add the ground almonds with the last few additions of egg, to prevent the mixture from separating. Sift the flour with the cornflour and baking powder. Using a large metal spoon, fold into the creamed mixture in batches alternately with the lemon juice. If necessary, add a little milk to make a soft dropping consistency. Spoon into the prepared tin and smooth the surface.

Bake in the preheated oven for 30 minutes, then reduce the oven temperature to 170C (325F, Gas 3) and bake for a further 1–1^1/$_4$ hours or until well risen and springy to the touch. A skewer inserted into the centre should come out clean. (If baking a smaller cake, reduce the oven temperature to 150C (300F, Gas 2) and bake for a further 1–1^1/$_4$ hours.) If the cake seems to be browning too much, cover with a double sheet of greaseproof paper. Leave in the tin until completely cold before turning out. The cooled cake can now be covered in marzipan, or wrapped in fresh greaseproof paper and foil and kept for up to 5 days before covering.

To cover the cake in marzipan, first remove all your rings and bangles to prevent making marks and dents. Turn the cake upside down and place it in the centre of the cake board. Check that the top surface is level. Brush the cake all over with lemon curd. Lightly dust the work surface with sifted icing sugar, then knead the marzipan until smooth. Roll it out into a round large enough to cover the top and sides of the cake (use a piece of string to measure the distance up one side of the cake, across the top and then down the other side). As you roll, move the marzipan around to prevent it from sticking, but do not turn it over. Carefully wrap the marzipan around the rolling pin, then lift it over the cake. Gently unroll the marzipan so the edge just touches the board on the far side. Then continue unrolling the marzipan over the cake so it covers the cake evenly and touches the board all around. Using the palm of your hand, smooth the marzipan on the top surface, and down against the sides of the cake to make sure it is well fixed. Trim the excess marzipan flush with the board. Leave to dry for 1–2 days.

To cover the cake with icing, first remove all your rings and bangles.

Brush the marzipanned cake with a little sherry or brandy so the icing will stick. Knead the sugar paste until smooth, then roll it out and cover the cake as for the marzipan. If air bubbles form, prick them at one side with a pin, then gently rub the bubble to expel the air. With your palm, spotlessy clean and dry, smooth and polish the surface of the icing. Do not press too hard with your fingers or there will be dents in the icing. Set the iced cake aside in a cool dry place to dry for up to 3 days.

To finish the cake, decorate with fresh, silk or sugar flowers. If using fresh flowers, arrange on top or use a special holder or ring available from cake decorating shops, cook shops and some bakers; the flowers will wilt rapidly if pushed into the icing. Decorate the base of the cake where it meets the cake board with foliage, ribbons or piped icing. The cake will cut into 45 pieces, and is best eaten within a week of being baked.

LEMON CURD

INGREDIENTS

Makes about 450g (1lb)

110g (4oz) unsalted butter, diced

230g (8oz) caster sugar

the grated rind and juice of 2 large or 3 small unwaxed lemons

3 eggs, size 2, beaten

spotlessly clean, sterilised jars

Lemon curd is used here to stick the marzipan to the lemon-flavoured cake, but it can also be used to sandwich sponge cakes, to spread on scones (see page 34), or mixed with whipped cream as a filling for cakes and pastries such as mille-feuilles (page 146) or profiteroles (page 149).

Put the butter, sugar, and lemon rind and juice into the top of a non-aluminium double saucepan or into a saucepan set in a bain-marie – a roasting tin of boiling water. Cook, stirring constantly with a wooden spoon, until smooth and melted. Add the eggs and stir until very thick and opaque. If the mixture boils it will scramble, so avoid short cuts.

Spoon into prepared jars and leave until cold, then cover and store in the fridge until ready to use – up to 2 weeks

CHAPTER FIVE

PASTRIES

Pastry is not just the container for a wonderful
filling, its taste and texture should enhance the whole dish.
With the help of a food processor, superb pastry
is easy to achieve.

MAKING PASTRY SUCCESSFULLY

Rich shortcrust pastry is easy to roll and cut if it is chilled first.

Making pastry is the exact opposite of bread making – you don't want to develop the gluten in the flour, as this makes the dough elastic, so heavy-duty kneading and man-handling are to be avoided. Also, to prevent the finished pastry from being greasy or heavy, it is important that the fats do not begin to turn oily or melt as you work the mixture; so use them cold and firm straight from the fridge and work rapidly, handling the mixture as little as possible.

For years I thought of my perpetually cold hands as a nuisance until other cooks told me I was lucky – their hot hands, the bane of their lives, hindered pastry-making. Many now make pastry in the food processor as it cuts down on handling, though it is important to run the machine only until the dough just comes together: if over-processed, the dough will become oily and sticky.

To make shortcrust pastry by hand, first lightly toss the flour and any other dry ingredients with the fat so the pieces of fat are coated in flour. Then cut the fat into smaller pieces about the size of your little fingernail, using one or two round-bladed knives or a wire pastry cutter. Finally, gently rub the fat and flour between the fingertips (not the palm of your hand), a small quantity at a time, until there are no visible lumps of fat and the mixture resembles fine crumbs. As you work, lift your hands up to the rim of the bowl so the mixture will become aerated as it falls back down into the bowl.

Bind the mixture together with icy cold water, or another liquid, using only just enough to make a soft dough. If the dough is dry and hard it will be difficult to roll out and use, but if it is too wet and sticky it will be tough and heavy when baked. Once the dough comes together, turn it on to a lightly floured work surface and very gently and briefly knead the dough to make it smooth and even.

To make pastry in a food processor, combine the flour and any other dry ingredients in the food processor bowl. Add the pieces of fat and process for about a minute or just until the mixture forms fine crumbs. Then, with the motor running, pour in the water or other liquid through the feed tube. The mixture should clump together within a minute. Immediately the mixture clumps together, stop the machine to prevent over-working. If the mixture doesn't come together, add more water a teaspoon at a time. Turn the dough on to a lightly floured work surface and gently knead for a few seconds to form a smooth ball.

Rich pastry doughs, such as rich shortcrust and almond pastry, need to be chilled before rolling out. Plain shortcrust doesn't normally need chilling, unless the kitchen is hot or the pastry dough shows signs of becoming oily. Wrap in greaseproof paper and chill for 15–20 minutes or until firm enough to roll out. Chilling helps the dough to relax, but it is not the antidote to over-working.

Puff pastry, the richest of all the pastries, remains the biggest challenge. The only short cut is to use a food processor to make the initial dough – the *détrempe*. The tricky part, incorporating as much butter as flour, has to be achieved by rolling and folding the dough by hand in a very precise fashion. But be reassured – success comes with practise.

PREVIOUS PAGE A selection of mincepies.

SHORTCRUST PASTRY

Makes about 340g (12oz)

230g (8oz) plain flour

a large pinch of salt

60g (2oz) unsalted butter, chilled and diced

60g (2oz) lard or white vegetable fat, chilled and diced

about 3 tablespoons icy water to bind

This pastry, with its short and light crumbly texture, is the simplest to make and the most versatile to use. In its most basic form, plain shortcrust is a dough made from plain flour (the type labelled for use in cakes and pastry rather than bread), fat, a little salt and some cold water. The shortness of the pastry depends on the type of fat used and the way it is incorporated into the flour. Firm unsalted butter gives the best flavour, but a mixture of lard, or white vegetable fat, and butter gives the best texture – that important melt-in-the-mouth quality. Most cooks use one part fat to two of flour, that is 30g (1oz) fat to 60g (2oz) flour, the fat being made up of equal amounts of butter and lard or white fat.

To make the pastry dough by hand, sift the flour and salt into a mixing bowl. Add the diced fats and toss lightly until well coated in flour. Using a round-bladed knife, two knives or a wire pastry cutter, cut the fats into small pieces, then rub the fats into the flour with the very tips of your fingers.

When the whole mixture looks like fine crumbs, with no clumps of fat, gradually pour in the water while stirring with a round-bladed knife. Keep stirring until the dough comes together – this can take a couple of

1 ADD THE FATS TO THE FLOUR AND USE A ROUND-BLADED KNIFE TO CUT THE FATS INTO QUITE SMALL PIECES.

2 RUB THE FLOUR AND PIECES OF FAT TOGETHER USING YOUR FINGERTIPS, LIFTING THE MIXTURE AS YOU RUB.

3 WHEN THE MIXTURE RESEMBLES FINE CRUMBS, SLOWLY ADD JUST ENOUGH COLD WATER TO BIND TO A DOUGH.

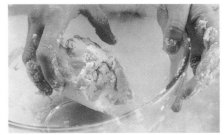

4 GATHER THE DOUGH TOGETHER IN YOUR HANDS AND FINISH BY MIXING BRIEFLY ON A FLOURED WORK SURFACE.

minutes. If any dry crumbs still remain at the bottom of the bowl, add more water a few drops at a time. The dough should hold together and be on the firm side of soft. If the dough is sticky or wet, stir in extra flour a little at a time. Turn on to a floured work surface and use your hand to bring the dough together to form a ball – try not to handle or work the dough too much as you don't want the fats to begin to melt and make the pastry oily. If this does happen, wrap the dough in greaseproof paper and chill for 15–20 minutes or until firm but not hard.

Alternatively, make the dough in a food processor (see page 132).

Roll out the dough on a lightly floured work surface, using a lightly floured rolling pin. Carefully lift and move the dough from time to time during rolling to check it is not sticking to the work surface; dust with extra flour as necessary.

1 PROCESS THE FATS AND FLOUR TOGETHER TO A CRUMB-LIKE TEXTURE.

2 ONCE WATER IS ADDED, THE DOUGH WILL COME TOGETHER IN A CLUMP.

RICH SHORTCRUST PASTRY

INGREDIENTS

Makes about 450g (1lb)
230g (8oz) plain flour
a large pinch of salt
60g (2oz) caster or icing sugar
170g (6oz) unsalted butter, chilled and diced
1 egg yolk, size 2
a little icy water to bind as necessary

Increasing the proportion of fat to flour — from half fat to flour to three-quarters fat to flour — makes the pastry taste richer. It also makes it slightly more difficult to work, so here the food processor is a blessing. Sugar, either caster or icing sugar, added before or after the fat is rubbed in, makes the pastry crisper as well as sweeter, but it also increases the risk of scorching during baking. Instead of water an egg yolk binds the dough and adds additional richness and colour — just the yolk is used as egg white tends to make pastry tough. Rich shortcrust is made in the same way as shortcrust pastry but needs to be chilled before rolling out.

To make the pastry dough by hand, sift the flour, salt and sugar into a mixing bowl. Add the diced butter and rub in with your fingertips until the mixture resembles fine crumbs. Stir in the egg yolk using a round-bladed knife; if necessary add a little icy water to bind the mixture and make a dough that is not too soft and neither sticky nor hard and dry. Wrap the dough in greaseproof paper and chill for 15–20 minutes or until firm but not hard.

Alternatively, make the dough in a food processor (see page 132).

To use, roll out as for shortcrust pastry.

1 TAKE THE BUTTER STRAIGHT FROM THE FRIDGE AND DICE IT QUICKLY BEFORE ADDING TO THE FLOUR AND SUGAR.

2 AFTER MIXING IN THE EGG YOLK AND WATER, STOP THE MACHINE AS SOON AS THE DOUGH COMES TOGETHER.

ALMOND PASTRY

Makes about 530g (1lb 3oz)
230g (8oz) plain flour
a large pinch of salt
40g (1½oz) ground almonds
85g (3oz) icing or caster sugar
170g (6oz) unsalted butter, chilled and diced
1 egg yolk, size 2

The addition of ground almonds gives rich shortcrust pastry an even richer flavour, and a good crumbly, light texture. I like to use this pastry for fruit tarts and flans as well as for mincepies. The sugar can be either icing sugar — which gives the pastry a fine, crisp texture — or caster, which makes it slightly more crumbly. Again, I prefer to make the dough in the food processor.

To make the pastry by hand, sift the flour, salt, ground almonds and sugar into a mixing bowl. Add the diced butter and cut into the flour mixture using a round-bladed knife. When the butter has been reduced to small flakes, use your fingertips to rub it into the flour. When the mixture looks like fine crumbs, stir in the egg yolk using a round-bladed knife to make a soft but not sticky dough. If there are dry crumbs left at the bottom of the bowl, add icy water a few drops at a time. Wrap the dough in greaseproof paper and chill for 15–20 minutes or until firm but not hard.

Alternatively, make the dough in a food processor (see page 132).

To use, roll out as for shortcrust pastry.

FOR THE BEST TEXTURE SIFT THE GROUND ALMONDS WITH THE FLOUR, SUGAR AND SALT TO REMOVE ANY LUMPS.

MINCEPIES

INGREDIENTS

Makes 12

1 batch shortcrust, rich shortcrust or almond pastry dough (pages 133-135)
340–450g (12oz–1lb) mincemeat (see recipe opposite)
caster or icing sugar for sprinkling

an 8 or 9cm (3¼ or 3⅝in) and a 6.5cm (2⅝in) plain or fluted round biscuit or scone cutter (see note below)
a small star, leaf or tree-shaped cutter (optional)
mincepie or bun tins, 6.5cm (2⅝in) diameter

Just as locally grown asparagus is even more of a treat because it is only in season for a few weeks in May, so the first mincepie tastes best because I know it is Christmas Eve. To fill me with seasonal cheer, just shut me in the kitchen with a batch of pastry and a few jars of home-made mincemeat, and the Festival of Nine Carols and Lessons from King's College on the radio.

Mincepies can be made with shortcrust, rich shortcrust or, my absolute favourite, almond pastry – I find puff pastry a bit too rich. Or you can use ready-made sheets of phyllo.

Preheat the oven to 180C (350F, Gas 4).

Roll out the pastry dough on a floured work surface to about 4mm (⅙in) thick. Cut out 12 rounds using the larger cutter and 12 rounds using the smaller cutter, re-rolling the trimmings as necessary. Line the tins with the larger rounds, gently pressing the dough against the sides of the tins with your thumb to remove any air bubbles. Put 1½–2 teaspoons of mincemeat in the centre of each pastry case.

Dampen the edges of the pastry cases using a pastry brush dipped in cold water. Cover with the smaller rounds and seal the edges by gently pressing down with an upside-down round cutter or small glass that just fits inside the rim of the tin. Make a small steam hole in the centre of each lid using a skewer.

If you like, cut a star, leaf or Christmas tree shape out of the centre of the smaller rounds before using to cover the pies. Alternatively, the pies can be decorated with shapes cut from the pastry trimmings – stick these on to the lids by dampening the undersides.

Bake the pies for 25–30 minutes or until firm and just golden – the richer pastries tend to brown very quickly so keep an eye on them. Leave to cool in the tins for several minutes. When the pastry firms up enough to allow the pies to be unmoulded, transfer them to a wire rack. Serve warm or at room temperature, dusted with caster or icing sugar, with brandy butter, cream or ice-cream. When completely cold, store in an airtight tin and eat within 5 days, or freeze.

NOTE Mincepie tins come in two depths, both with the same diameter, so the size of cutter needed for the dough rounds to line the tins will depend on the depth.

1 LIGHTLY MOISTEN THE RIMS OF THE PASTRY CASES WITH COLD WATER BEFORE COVERING WITH THE LIDS.

2 TO SEAL THE PIES, GENTLY PRESS DOWN WITH AN UPTURNED CUTTER THAT IS SLIGHTLY SMALLER THAN THE TIN.

LUXURIOUS MINCEMEAT

INGREDIENTS

Makes about 1.35kg (3lb)

230g (8oz) currants

230g (8oz) large seedless raisins

85g (3oz) mixed candied peel, finely chopped

60g (2oz) stem ginger, drained of syrup, chopped

110g (4oz) cooking apple, peeled, cored and grated

110g (4oz) shredded beef suet or vegetarian suet

30g (1oz) blanched almonds, chopped

30g (1oz) walnut pieces, chopped

the grated rind and juice of $^1/_2$ unwaxed orange

the grated rind and juice of $^1/_2$ unwaxed lemon

170g (6oz) dark muscovado sugar

$^1/_2$ teaspoon each ground cinnamon, grated nutmeg and ground mixed spice

140ml (5fl oz) brandy or ginger wine

sterilised jars and lids

Christmas Eve — mincepies, mulled wine, and an aromatic log fire.

RIGHT *A snow-covered church in Bavaria.*

I like mincemeat to be fruity and moist but not too sweet, and nicely steeped in brandy. The nuts add a crunchy texture as well as improving the balance of flavours. Mincemeat can also be used to make an easy fruit cake (see page 110) or to fill a large double crust pie or Jalousie (see page 142).

Put all the ingredients into a large mixing bowl and mix thoroughly. Cover tightly and leave to stand in a cool spot for a day to allow the flavours to infuse and blend. Stir from time to time.

Give the mincemeat a good mix, then spoon into the prepared jars. Cover and leave in the fridge or a cold place for several weeks to allow the mincemeat to mature. Before using, stir well. Always store opened jars in the fridge.

SHORTBREAD-TOPPED MINCEPIES

INGREDIENTS

Makes 20

1 batch shortcrust, rich shortcrust or almond pastry
  dough (pages 133-135)
about 450g (1lb) mincemeat (page 137)

TOPPING:
170g (6oz) unsalted butter, at room temperature
60g (2oz) golden caster sugar
170g (6oz) plain flour
110g (4oz) ground almonds

an 8 or 9cm (3¼ or 3⅝in) plain or fluted round
  biscuit cutter
mincepie or bun tins, 6.5cm (2⅝in) diameter
a piping bag fitted with a large star tube

These mincepies are lighter than they appear, and disappear even faster than ordinary mincepies. Although the bases can be made from shortcrust or rich shortcrust, almond pastry is the most delicious when combined with good mincemeat and this rich, but not sweet, almond shortbread mixture piped on top.

Preheat the oven to 180C (350F, Gas 4).

Roll out the pastry dough fairly thinly and cut out 20 rounds using the biscuit cutter (according to the depth of your tins), re-rolling the trimmings as necessary. Use to line the mincepie or bun tins. Put 1½–2 teaspoons of mincemeat into each pastry case.

To make the topping, beat the butter with the sugar until light and fluffy, then mix in the flour and the almonds. Use your hands to bring the mixture together, kneading gently until smooth; it should be just soft enough to pipe. Spoon the mixture into the piping bag fitted with the star tube and pipe a swirl on the top of each mincemeat-filled pastry case. Chill for 5 minutes.

Bake for 25–30 minutes or until a light golden brown. Leave to cool slightly in the tins. When the pastry is firm enough to unmould, transfer the pies carefully to a wire rack. Eat warm or at room temperature, plain or with cream or ice-cream. When completely cold, store in an airtight tin and eat within 5 days, or freeze.

PHYLLO MINCEPIES

INGREDIENTS

Makes about 16

125g (4½oz) phyllo pastry, about 8 sheets
110g (4oz) unsalted butter, melted
340–450g (12oz –1lb) mincemeat (page 137)
icing sugar for dusting

mincepie or bun tins. 6.5 cm (2⅝in) diameter

I first discovered these on a visit to The Walnut Tree Inn, near Abergavenny in South Wales. Watching the chef and proprietor, Franco Taruschio, make petit-four mincepies to serve with coffee at Christmas was a revelation – the quickest, lightest, crunchiest mincepies can be made from phyllo pastry. The pastry is simply cut into squares, brushed with melted butter and then used to line the tins and to cover the mincemeat filling.

Preheat the oven to 180C (350F, Gas 4).

If the pastry is frozen, thaw according to the packet instructions. Once unwrapped, keep the pastry covered with cling film or a damp tea towel to prevent it from drying out. Lay one sheet of pastry on the work surface. Cut the sheet into 7.5cm (3in) squares using a large sharp knife or kitchen scissors (if your tins are deep, cut slightly larger squares) and brush them with melted butter. Use three squares, arranged at different angles, to line each mincepie tin, and lightly press into the bottom. The pastry will hang over the rim of the tin.

Put 1½–2 teaspoons of mincemeat in the centre of each pastry case. Cover with another two squares of pastry, crumpled lightly like a scarf.

Bake for 8–10 minutes or until a good golden brown and crisp. Remove from the tins and cool on a wire rack. Serve warm or at room temperature, dusted with sifted icing sugar. Store the mincepies in an airtight tin, and eat them within 2 days.

1 USING A PASTRY BRUSH, COAT THE CUT SQUARES OF PHYLLO WITH A THIN LAYER OF MELTED BUTTER.

2 LINE EACH TIN WITH THREE SQUARES OF BUTTERED PHYLLO, ARRANGING THEM AT SLIGHTLY DIFFERENT ANGLES.

3 SPOON A LITTLE MINCEMEAT INTO THE CENTRE OF EACH PHYLLO-LINED TIN, WITHOUT OVERFILLING.

4 COVER EACH PIE WITH TWO MORE SQUARES OF BUTTERED PASTRY, CRUMPLED UP LIKE A CHIFFON SCARF.

LEFT Franco Taruschio making his perfect mincepies in his kitchen at The Walnut Tree Inn.

QUEEN MARY TARTLETS

INGREDIENTS

Makes 12
PASTRY:
110g (4oz) plain flour
a pinch of salt
70g (2¹/₂oz) margarine, butter or a mix of fats, chilled and diced
¹/₂ teaspoon caster sugar
1 egg yolk
2 teaspoons icy water

FILLING:
60g (2oz) margarine or butter, at room temperature
60g (2oz) caster sugar
1 egg, size 2
110g (4oz) sultanas
30g (1oz) mixed candied peel, finely chopped

an 8 cm (3¹/₄in) plain or fluted round biscuit cutter
tartlet or shallow mincepie tins, 6.5cm (2⁵/₈in) diameter

Another Scottish recipe from Katie Stewart (see page 112) — simple, sweet, fruit-filled tartlets dating back to the court of Mary Queen of Scots. The pastry can be made with margarine, butter, or a mixture of either with lard or white vegetable fat.

Preheat the oven to 190C (375F, Gas 5).

Make the pastry: sift the flour and salt into a mixing bowl, add the fat and rub in with your fingertips until the mixture looks like fine crumbs. Stir in the sugar. Mix together the egg yolk and water, then stir into the mixture to make a firm dough.

Roll out the dough fairly thinly on a lightly floured work surface. Cut out 12 rounds using the biscuit cutter, re-rolling the trimmings as necessary. Use the rounds to line the tartlet or mincepie tins, pressing the dough gently against the bottom and sides of the tins to eliminate any air bubbles. Try not to stretch the dough as you do this.

For the filling, beat the margarine or butter with the sugar until light and fluffy, then beat in the egg. When thoroughly blended, stir in the sultanas and the chopped candied peel. Divide the filling equally among the tartlet cases and smooth the surface.

Bake for 15–20 minutes or until the pastry under the filling is cooked – to test, carefully loosen and lift out the filling from one tartlet using a small round-bladed knife. Remove the tartlets from the tins and leave to cool on a baking tray. Eat warm or at room temperature, within 24 hours of baking.

ROUGH PUFF PASTRY

INGREDIENTS

Makes about 340g (12oz)
230g (8oz) plain flour
¼ teaspoon salt
60g (2oz) butter, chilled and finely diced
60g (2oz) lard or white vegetable fat, chilled and
    finely diced
about 4 tablespoons icy water to bind

Rough puff is quicker, simpler and less rich than puff pastry, but it still has plenty of layers of crisp, light pastry, and it is ideal for deep fruit pies as well as tarts and flans. Although you can use all butter for a richer taste, I find a combination of butter and lard or white vegetable fat helps the dough to rise more during baking and makes a lighter pastry. To make rough puff, flakes of fat are combined with flour and water to make a soft lumpy dough, which is then rolled out and folded six times, just as with puff pastry. This incorporates the fat into the dough in hundreds of layers.

Sift the flour and salt into a mixing bowl. Add the cold diced fats and stir gently with a round-bladed knife until they are thoroughly coated in flour. Stir in enough icy water to bind the dough, adding it a tablespoon at a time. The dough should be lumpy, soft and moist, but not sticky or wet.

Turn the dough on to a lightly floured work surface and form it into a brick shape by gently patting with floured fingers. Using a floured rolling pin, roll out the dough away from you into a rectangle 45 x 15cm (18 x 6in). Fold the dough in three like a business letter: fold the bottom third of the dough up to cover the centre third, then fold the top third down to cover the other two layers. Gently but firmly seal the edges by pressing down with the rolling pin. This is the first 'turn'.

Lift up the piece of dough and give it a quarter turn anti-clockwise, so that the folded edges are now at the sides. Roll out and fold in three again, just as before, then give the dough a quarter turn anti-clockwise; repeat. After this third 'turn', wrap the dough and chill for 20 minutes, then do three more 'turns', to make a total of six. Chill for 20 minutes before using.

1 THE DOUGH SHOULD LOOK LUMPY, SOFT AND MOIST BUT NOT WET OR STICKY.

2 SHAPE THE DOUGH INTO A BRICK, THEN ROLL IT OUT TO MAKE A RECTANGLE.

3 FOLD THE RECTANGLE OF DOUGH IN THREE LIKE A BUSINESS LETTER.

4 PRESS THE EDGES OF THE FOLDED DOUGH WITH THE ROLLING PIN TO SEAL THEM.

CARAMELISED MANGO JALOUSIE

Serves 4
1 batch rough puff pastry dough (page 141)
2 medium to large ripe mangoes
2 tablespoons caster sugar
2 pieces of stem ginger, drained of syrup, finely
   chopped (optional)

GLAZE:
a little egg white, lightly beaten, for brushing
1 tablespoon caster sugar for sprinkling

a baking tray, lightly greased

Instead of mangoes, you can use lightly poached, forced spring rhubarb for this delicious pastry. Other possible fillings include ripe cherries, stoned and tossed with sugar; quartered apricots; apple slices mixed with mincemeat; or some very good jam.

Heat the grill.

Wrap the prepared pastry dough and leave to rest in the fridge while making the filling (this will help the gluten in the flour to relax).

Peel the mangoes and cut the fruit away from the stone, taking two pieces from each mango. Slice each piece lengthways like a fan so the slices remain attached at one end. Arrange the four mango 'fans' on the prepared baking tray and sprinkle with the sugar. Grill for a few minutes or until the tops of the fruit become golden and caramelised. Remove and leave to cool completely.

Preheat the oven to 220C (425F, Gas 7).

On a lightly floured work surface, roll out the pastry dough to a rectangle 30.5 x 25.5cm (12 x 10in). Using a large sharp knife, trim the edges to make them straight, then cut the rectangle in half lengthways to

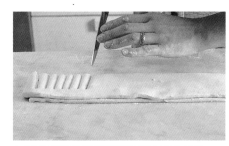

1 FOLD THE PASTRY STRIP IN HALF AND CUT SLITS ACROSS THE FOLD.

2 MOISTEN THE PASTRY EDGES USING A PASTRY BRUSH DIPPED IN COLD WATER.

3 'KNOCK UP' THE SIDE SO THE PASTRY WILL RISE EVENLY DURING BAKING.

make two long narrow strips. Cut cleanly without dragging the dough. Put one strip on the clean, greased baking tray. Lightly dust the other strip of dough with flour and fold it in half lengthways. Cut slits across the fold, about 1cm (³/₈in) apart, leaving an uncut border about 2cm (³/₄in) wide along the top, bottom and sides. When opened the strip should look like a Venetian blind or ladder.

Arrange the cold caramelised mango fans in a line down the centre of the strip of dough on the baking sheet. Scatter over the ginger, if using. Dampen the edges of the strip with a brush dipped in cold water. Lay the cut strip of dough on top and carefully unfold to cover the base and filling. Gently press the edges to seal, then trim to neaten. Using a small knife, 'knock up' the sides: hold the knife parallel to the assembled pastry and gently 'knock' the blade against the pastry sides to make a series of horizontal marks – the pastry sides will look like the closed pages of a book. Using two fingers and the small knife, flute the edges all around by gently pressing the fingertips down and drawing the knife up between them to form small scallops.

Chill the pastry for 5 minutes, then bake for 20 minutes or until golden and crisp. Remove the baking tray from the oven. Brush the jalousie lightly with egg white, then sprinkle with sugar. Return to the oven and bake for a further 5 minutes. Serve warm, with cream, ice-cream or fromage frais.

PUFF PASTRY

Makes about 600g (1lb 5oz)
250g (8³/₄oz) plain flour
¹/₂ teaspoon salt
250g (8³/₄oz) unsalted butter, cold
1 teaspoon lemon juice
about 125ml (4¹/₂fl oz) icy water

A selection of puff pastry confections and other tea-time treats at Betty's of Harrogate.

This, the lightest, richest, flakiest and most delicious of all pastries, is time-consuming to make and tricky to master. Oh, but the taste is worth it! Nothing can compare to its butteriness, for this pastry contains as much butter as flour, incorporated into the dough by rolling and folding six times, to form seemingly hundreds of airy layers. It makes a fine mille-feuilles layered with cream and fruit, or it can be used for chaussons (fruit turnovers) or a Pithiviers – a gâteau filled with a rich almond frangipane.

As with all pastry it is important to avoid developing the gluten in the flour (this is only desirable when making bread dough, where the resulting elasticity is essential). With puff pastry, over-working and stretching the dough would result in it shrinking alarmingly and becoming tough. Although lemon juice helps to prevent this, I prefer to make the détrempe – the initial dough – in the food processor, to cut down on handling, and I stick religiously to the chilling times.

The butter is most easily incorporated if it is cold – the same temperature as the détrempe – but pliable rather than hard. So I use it straight from the fridge and beat it with a rolling pin to get the right consistency. It is vital not to let the butter get warm and start to ooze out of the dough or the pastry will not rise during baking and will be end up greasy and heavy.

For convenience, the dough can be stored in the fridge for 4 days, or frozen, after you have given it four 'turns'. Then the last two 'turns' can be completed when you want to use the dough.

Sift the flour and salt and tip into the bowl of a food processor. Add 30g (1oz) of the butter, cut into dice, and process until the mixture resembles fine crumbs. Mix the lemon juice and water. With the machine running, pour the liquid in via the feed tube in a steady stream, to make a ball of soft dough that is fairly moist but not sticky or wet. If the dough seems dry or there are crumbs left in the bottom of the bowl, add a little extra water a teaspoon at a time. Turn the dough on to a lightly floured work surface and shape into a ball, then cut a deep cross in the top (this helps reduce the elasticity). Wrap and chill for 15 minutes.

Dust the remaining slab of butter with a little flour, then place it between two pieces of cling film. Pound with a rolling pin until the butter is half as thick as it was. Remove the film. Fold the butter in two, then place between the film and pound again. Keep pounding and folding in this way until the butter is pliable but not soft, then fold and beat the butter to make a square with 12.5cm (5in) long sides.

Set the ball of dough on a lightly floured work surface. Using a floured rolling pin, roll out the dough to make four flaps with a thick square of dough – the size of the square of butter – in the centre. Lift the dough and give it a quarter turn after rolling each flap. Put the square of butter, dusted with flour, on the central square of dough and fold the four flaps over the butter so it is completely enclosed. Gently press the seams to seal. Turn the piece of dough upside down, then lightly press with the rolling pin several times to flatten the dough – do this gently because the fat must not be forced out of its dough wrapping.

Lightly roll out the dough into a rectangle 45 x 15cm (18 x 6in), rolling away from your body in short brisk movements. Fold the dough in three like a business letter: fold the bottom third up to cover the centre third, then fold the top third down to cover the other two layers, making a neat square of dough. Lightly press the edges with the rolling pin to seal. This completes the first 'turn'.

Lift up the piece of dough and give it a quarter turn anti-clockwise, so that the folded edges are now at the sides. Roll out the dough into a rectangle and fold it in three again, just as before. Use two fingers to mark the dough with a couple of dents, to indicate that it has had two 'turns', then wrap the dough and chill for 15 minutes.

Give the dough two more 'turns', and mark with four little indentations. Wrap and chill the dough as before. At this point the pastry can be stored in the fridge for 4 days or frozen. Before using, give the dough two more 'turns', to make a total of six.

1 DUST THE SLAB OF CHILLED BUTTER WITH FLOUR, THEN POUND WITH THE ROLLING PIN UNTIL PLIABLE BUT FIRM.

2 ROLL OUT THE BALL OF DOUGH IN FOUR DIRECTIONS TO MAKE FOUR FLAPS WITH A THICK SQUARE IN THE CENTRE.

3 SET THE FLOURED BUTTER SQUARE IN THE CENTRE AND FOLD THE FLAPS OF DOUGH OVER TO ENCLOSE IT.

4 LIGHTLY PRESS THE SQUARE OF DOUGH WITH THE ROLLING PIN TO FLATTEN IT, THEN ROLL OUT INTO A RECTANGLE.

5 FOLD THE RECTANGLE IN THREE – THE BOTTOM THIRD UP, THEN THE TOP THIRD DOWN – TO MAKE A SQUARE SHAPE.

6 MAKE DENTS IN THE PASTRY WITH YOUR FINGERS AS A REMINDER OF HOW MANY 'TURNS' YOU'VE COMPLETED.

MILLE FEUILLES

INGREDIENTS

Serves 6–8

$^1/_2$ batch puff pastry dough (page 144), about 300g (10$^1/_2$oz)

3–4 tablespoons good raspberry jam

140ml (5fl oz) double cream, chilled and whipped

150g (about 5oz) raspberries

icing sugar for dusting

a large baking tray, lightly greased

This recipe shows off puff pastry to its best advantage — it is simply baked in a sheet, then sliced into three and layered with cream and fruit. You can use a variety of fillings to suit the season: pastry cream (see recipe page 166) instead of whipped fresh cream, strawberries, fresh sliced peaches or apricots, stoned cherries, fresh currants, or lightly poached and well-drained fruit like rhubarb or pears. Once assembled, eat as soon as possible because the pastry quickly becomes soggy.

Preheat the oven to 220C (425F, Gas 7).

Roll out the pastry dough to a square with 30.5cm (12in) sides, then trim the edges to straighten them using a large sharp knife. Avoid dragging the knife or pulling the dough as this will distort the shape. Put the square of dough upside down on the prepared baking tray and prick the dough all over with a fork.

Bake for 10 minutes or until well risen, golden and crisp. Remove from the oven and cool on a wire rack.

Cut the cold pastry into three equal rectangles, measuring 10 x 30.5cm (4 x 12in). If necessary, trim the sides to neaten them. Put one pastry rectangle on a serving plate and spread with the jam, then cover with half of the whipped cream. Spread the rest of the whipped cream on a second pastry rectangle and place this on top. Arrange the fruit on the cream very gently, then cover with the third rectangle of pastry. Dust with sifted icing sugar, and serve.

CHOUX PASTRY

INGREDIENTS

Makes a 3-egg quantity
110g (4oz) plain flour
185ml (6½fl oz) water from the cold tap
a large pinch of salt
75g (2½oz) unsalted butter, diced
3 eggs, beaten

Unlike shortcrust and other rubbed-in pastries, choux is cooked in a saucepan before it is baked in the oven. The soft dough — made from butter, water, flour, salt and egg — is piped or dropped in spoonfuls on to a baking tray. In the oven it rises and puffs up to make a crisp hollow container. Choux pastry is used for éclairs and profiteroles to be filled with pastry cream (crème pâtissière), whipped cream or ice-cream, or beignets, which are deep-fried fritters served with a fruit sauce.

To make successful choux pastry it is important to measure the ingredients very carefully and accurately. In addition, the water must not boil and begin to evaporate before the butter in it has melted. The eggs should be added gradually because if too little is beaten into the dough it will be hard and flat; if too much is added the dough will be too soft to pipe and will not hold a shape.

Sift the flour on to a piece of paper. Put the water, salt and butter into a medium-sized saucepan and heat gently until the butter has completely melted. Rapidly bring the mixture to the boil, then immediately remove from the heat and tip in all the flour. Beat vigorously with a wooden spoon — the mixture will look a complete mess and a failure at the start but will come together to make a smooth, heavy clump of dough. Return the pan to a low heat and beat the dough for half a minute to dry it slightly. It should come away from the sides of the pan to form a smooth ball.

Turn the dough into a large mixing bowl and leave to cool until tepid. Then, using an electric mixer — you can use a wooden spoon if you prefer, but it is hard work — gradually beat in the eggs, beating well after each addition. Beat in just enough egg to make a smooth and shiny paste-like dough that falls from the spoon when lightly shaken. Keep covered until ready to use.

1 DO NOT LET THE *WATER* BOIL BEFORE THE BUTTER *HAS* COMPLETELY MELTED.

2 OFF THE HEAT, BEAT IN THE FLOUR VIGOROUSLY USING *A WOODEN* SPOON.

3 RETURN TO *A LOW HEAT AND* BEAT THE DOUGH TO DRY IT SLIGHTLY.

4 BEAT IN JUST ENOUGH EGG TO MAKE *A* FAIRLY STIFF PASTE-LIKE DOUGH.

TINY ÉCLAIRS

Clare Cave, a friend who caters parties for the Duke of Westminster and up, cooked the most heavenly food for my wedding party, but I can only remember eating the miniature, lighter than air, utterly delicious éclairs. The finger-size choux pastry cases must be well-cooked and crisp before they are filled, otherwise they quickly become soggy. Whipped cream, chocolate mousse (see the Chocolate Macaroons on page 24) or pastry cream can be used to fill them — here I've used coffee pastry cream, and coated the tops with a coffee glacé icing. Eat as soon as possible after assembling.

Preheat the oven to 190C (375F, Gas 5).

For éclairs, choux paste should hold its own shape and be stiff enough to pipe, so add the last spoonfuls of egg very slowly. Spoon the choux paste into the piping bag fitted with the plain tube and pipe éclairs the size of your little finger on the prepared baking trays. Space the éclairs well apart to allow for rising and spreading.

Bake for 20 minutes or until crisp and golden. Remove from the oven, and make a small hole in one end of each éclair using a skewer or cocktail stick to let out the steam. Return the éclairs to the oven and bake for a further 3–4 minutes. Cool on a wire rack.

To make the pastry cream, beat the egg yolks with the sugar in a heatproof mixing bowl until light and creamy. (To avoid spills set the bowl on a damp cloth.) Sift in the flour and cornflour and mix until smooth. Heat the milk in a heavy saucepan until scalding hot, then add the coffee and stir until dissolved. Pour on to the egg mixture, stirring briskly to make a smooth, creamy liquid. Tip into the rinsed-out saucepan and cook, stirring constantly, until the mixture boils, then beat vigorously until smooth. Turn into a bowl and rub the surface with a little butter to prevent a skin from forming, then leave to cool.

Spoon the cold pastry cream into the clean, dry piping bag fitted with the plain tube. Pipe into the éclairs through one end by enlarging the steam hole.

For the coffee glacé icing, put the sifted sugar into a small mixing bowl and stir in the hot coffee to make a smooth icing. Dip the top of each filled éclair in the icing and leave to set. Eat within 4 hours.

1 PIPE THE ÉCLAIRS, CUTTING THE DOUGH OFF NEATLY WITH A SMALL KNIFE.

2 TO ENSURE CRISP PASTRY, MAKE A SMALL STEAM-HOLE IN EACH BAKED ÉCLAIR.

VARIATIONS: CHOCOLATE ÉCLAIRS Omit the coffee in the pastry cream. Melt 100g (3½oz) good dark chocolate and add to the cooked pastry cream, off the heat, before transferring it to the bowl. Replace the coffee powder in the icing with 1 tablespoon sifted cocoa powder.

PROFITEROLES Put the choux pastry into the piping bag fitted with the plain tube and pipe rounded mounds about 2.5cm (1in) wide and 1.2cm (½in) high on to the prepared baking trays. Lightly brush with beaten egg, making sure that it does not drip down and glue the pastry to the tray. Bake as above. When cold, fill with coffee, vanilla or chocolate pastry cream, whipped cream or, my favourite, vanilla ice-cream. Serve with a sauce – chocolate, caramel or fruit, depending on the filling.

LEFT Rena Salaman works rapidly to assemble her baklava.

ABOVE The finished baklava (see recipe on next page).

PHYLLO PASTRY

These wafer-thin sheets of pastry, spelled phyllo or filo, are now used for all kinds of sweet and savoury dishes. Traditional Greek baklava (see page 152) and mincepies (page 139) are just two delicious examples. Strudel, pastis and brik doughs are similar to phyllo, though slightly thicker; all become crisp, light and flaky when baked.

While you can make strudel and pastis doughs at home – kneading, stretching, rolling and pulling a soft and very pliable dough of flour, egg and water to make a sheet so thin you can read the newspaper through it – phyllo is always bought ready made. Most supermarkets and delis sell frozen brands. The quality of frozen phyllo varies from the abysmal to the wonderful, and I have been disappointed many times, so I asked the Greek cook and food expert, Rena Salaman, for advice. She recommends the Antoniou brand available from some supermarkets and delis.

When using frozen phyllo, it is important to follow the instructions on the packet. Thawing should be at room temperature, and once thawed and unwrapped the pastry sheets must be kept covered with a damp tea towel or cling film while you are working on the recipe. If the pastry dries out, it hardens, cracks and crumbles and becomes almost impossible to fold.

RENA'S BAKLAVA

INGREDIENTS

Cuts into about 24 pieces

500g (1lb 2oz) phyllo pastry

380g (13¹/₂oz) walnut pieces, coarsely chopped
(see recipe)

2 tablespoons caster sugar

1 teaspoon ground cinnamon

185g (6¹/₂oz) unsalted butter, melted

2 tablespoons water from the cold tap

SYRUP:

330g (11³/₄oz) granulated or caster sugar

300ml (10¹/₂fl oz) water

1–2 cinnamon sticks, depending on their size and
your taste

2 teaspoons lemon juice

3 tablespoons clear honey, preferably Greek and
thyme-scented

a roasting tin, about 30.5cm (12in) in diameter if
round or 37 x 25cm (14¹/₂ x 9³/₄in) if
rectangular (see recipe)

This is a real mouth-opener, and nothing like commercial baklava. The recipe comes from the distinguished Greek cook and food writer, Rena Salaman. It is made with commercial phyllo pastry, plenty of walnuts and some cinnamon. Other cooks use pistachios or almonds, but Rena prefers walnuts because they have a greater depth of flavour and a little sharpness to counterbalance the sugar syrup. No special equipment is needed as Rena bakes the baklava in a roasting tin.

If the pastry is frozen, thaw according to packet instructions. Once unwrapped, keep it covered with cling film or a damp tea towel to prevent it from drying out.

Preheat the oven to 180C (350F, Gas 4).

The walnuts should be chopped to the consistency of coarse breadcrumbs. Mix them with the sugar and cinnamon in a bowl. Set aside.

Unfold the phyllo sheets and choose a roasting tin that best fits their shape: round or rectangular. The sizes of tins suggested usually fit almost perfectly, but you can use other size tins and then just fold in the edges of the phyllo sheets a little. Using a pastry brush, grease the tin liberally with melted butter to prevent sticking.

Cover the bottom of the tin neatly with a sheet of phyllo and brush it with butter. Continue adding sheets, buttering each one. When you have layered about six sheets of phyllo, spread with about a third of the walnut

1 BRUSH THE PHYLLO SHEETS WITH BUTTER BEFORE OR AFTER ARRANGING THEM IN THE TIN, AS YOU WISH.

2 WHEN THERE ARE SIX SHEETS IN THE TIN, SPRINKLE IN A THIRD OF THE WALNUT FILLING AND SPREAD EVENLY.

3 COVER WITH TWO MORE BUTTERED PHYLLO SHEETS BEFORE ADDING MORE OF THE WALNUT FILLING.

4 AFTER ADDING THE FINAL LAYER OF FILLING, FOLD IN THE EDGES OF THE PHYLLO SHEETS OVER THE SURFACE.

filling. Cover with two more sheets of buttered phyllo and spread with half of the remaining filling. Place two sheets of buttered phyllo on top and spread evenly with the rest of the filling. Fold in the edges of the phyllo sheets all around to enclose the filling, rather like a parcel. Place the remaining phyllo on top, buttering each sheet before lifting it. Trim the excess pastry around the edges using a small knife or a pair of scissors – remember that phyllo pastry tends to shrink so do not trim too much.

Now comes the tricky part. Phyllo pastry is too brittle to be cut neatly after it has been baked, so the pieces have to be cut before it goes into the oven. Using a sharp knife cut the baklava carefully into oblong pieces. Ideally the pieces should be the same size, but if not it is not the end of the world. Sprinkle the cold water all over the surface with your fingertips: the moisture will prevent the pastry edges curling up in the oven.

Bake in the preheated oven for 15 minutes, then turn up the temperature to 190C (375F, Gas 5) and bake for a further 15–20 minutes or until the surface is crisp and light golden. Remove from the oven and leave to cool while you make the syrup.

Put the sugar and water in a saucepan and heat, stirring, until the sugar dissolves, then bring to the boil. Add the remaining ingredients, cover and simmer for about 10 minutes to make a light, syrupy consistency. Remove from the heat and let the syrup stand for 10 minutes.

Pour the syrup slowly through a fine sieve over all of the warm baklava. Leave it to absorb all the syrup. The baklava is delicious freshly made, but it will also keep well for 3–4 days, covered tightly with cling film.

5 AFTER COVERING WITH THE REST OF THE PASTRY, TRIM OFF THE EXCESS AT THE EDGE WITH A SHARP KNIFE.

6 CUT THROUGH THE BAKLAVA TO MARK OUT SMALL SQUARES OR OBLONGS, THEN SPRINKLE WITH WATER AND BAKE.

7 ONCE THE SUGAR HAS DISSOLVED, BRING THE SYRUP TO THE BOIL AND ADD THE CINNAMON, JUICE AND HONEY.

8 LET THE SYRUP COOL SLIGHTLY BEFORE POURING IT, THROUGH A SIEVE, EVENLY OVER THE WARM BAKLAVA.

CHAPTER SIX

PIES & TARTS

Making a clear distinction between a pie and a
tart isn't easy: both have a pastry base and a
filling, but both may also have a pastry cover
or other topping. Whatever you call them,
the case and its contents should not
merely share a plate — they ought
to make a good marriage.

LEMON MERINGUE PIE

INGREDIENTS

Makes a 20.5cm (8in) pie, to serve 6
PASTRY:
170g (6oz) plain flour
a pinch of salt
20g (³/₄oz) caster sugar
110g (4oz) unsalted butter, chilled and diced
1 egg yolk, mixed with 2 teaspoons icy water

FILLING:
the grated rind and juice of 3 large unwaxed lemons
40g (1¹/₂oz) cornflour
280ml (10fl oz) water
2 egg yolks
85g (3oz) caster sugar
45g (1¹/₂oz) unsalted butter, diced

MERINGUE TOPPING:
3 egg whites
140g (5oz) caster sugar

a 20.5cm (8in) loose-based flan tin

It may be corny, but this is my favourite dessert. The lemon filling is nicely sharp and well-flavoured, and unlike most recipes it is made rich and creamy with butter. To keep the pastry base from going soggy, bake it thoroughly before adding the filling. If you cannot find unwaxed lemons, give the fruit a good scrub with hot soapy water before grating the rind.

Note that the recipe uses three eggs: one yolk for the pastry, the other two yolks for the filling, and the three whites for the meringue topping.

Make the pastry: sift the flour and salt into a mixing bowl and stir in the sugar. Add the diced butter and rub into the dry ingredients, using the tips of your fingers, until the mixture resembles fine crumbs. Using a round-bladed knife, stir in the egg yolk mixture to make a slightly firm dough – it should not be dry and crumbly nor soft and sticky. The dough can also be made in a food processor (see page 132). Chill the dough until firm – about 15 minutes.

Turn the dough on to a lightly floured work surface and knead for a couple of seconds or until smooth. Roll out to a round about 26.5cm (10 ¹/₂in) in diameter. Roll the dough up around the rolling pin and lift it over the flan tin. Gently unroll the dough so it drapes over the tin. Carefully press the dough on to the bottom of the tin and up the sides so there are no pockets of air. Roll the pin over the top of the tin to cut off the excess dough.

The sides of the pastry case should stand slightly above the rim of the flan tin, just in case the pastry shrinks during baking. So use your thumbs to press and ease the pastry sides upwards to make a neat rim that is about 6mm (¹/₄in) higher than the tin. Curve your fore-finger inside this rim and gently press the pastry over your finger so the rim curves inwards

1 ROLL THE DOUGH AROUND THE ROLLING PIN AND LIFT IT OVER THE FLAN TIN.

2 CUT OFF THE EXCESS DOUGH BY ROLLING THE PIN OVER THE TOP OF THE TIN.

3 POUR THE HOT FILLING INTO THE BAKED PASTRY CASE AND SPREAD EVENLY.

4 SPOON THE MERINGUE ON TOP AND SPREAD GENTLY WITH A KNIFE.

PREVIOUS PAGE Summer Fruit Tart.

rather than over-hanging the rim of the tin. (This makes unmoulding easier.) The pastry rim can be fluted with your fingers to match the fluting of the tin sides. Prick the bottom of the pastry case all over with a fork to prevent the pastry from bubbling up during baking. Chill for 10–15 minutes or until firm.

Preheat the oven to 200C (400F, Gas 6).

Bake the pastry case blind (see page 158). Remove from the oven and leave to cool slightly while you make the filling. Leave the oven on at 180C (350F, Gas 4).

Put the grated lemon rind and juice into a small heatproof bowl with the cornflour. Add 2 tablespoons of the water and stir well. Bring the rest of the water to the boil in a medium-sized saucepan. Pour the boiling water on to the cornflour mixture, stirring constantly, then tip the contents of the bowl into the saucepan. Cook, stirring constantly, until the mixture boils. Reduce the heat and simmer for 2 minutes to make smooth, thick paste. Remove from the heat and beat in the egg yolks and sugar, then the butter. When thoroughly combined and there are no streaks in the mixture, spoon it into the pastry case.

To make the meringue topping, put the egg whites into a non-plastic, spotlessly clean, grease-free bowl and whisk until soft peaks form. Gradually whisk in the sugar, then whisk well to make a stiff shiny meringue. Spoon the meringue over the lemon filling to cover completely, spreading it out gently.

Bake for 15–20 minutes or until the meringue is just firm and a good golden brown. Serve at room temperature, within 24 hours of baking.

HOW TO BAKE BLIND

FILL THE PAPER-LINED PASTRY CASE WITH A LAYER OF CERAMIC OR DRIED BEANS.

Cut a round of non-stick baking parchment about the same size as the round of pastry dough used to line the tin. Crumple up the paper, then open it out and gently press it into the pastry case to cover the bottom and sides – this is easy if the pastry is chilled and firm. It is important to press the paper into the angle where the sides meet the bottom. Fill the paper-lined case with enough ceramic baking beans, dried beans, uncooked rice or dry bread crusts to weigh it down. Bake the pastry case in a preheated 200C (400F, Gas 6) oven for 15 minutes or until lightly golden and just firm. Carefully remove the paper and beans, lower the oven temperature to 180C (350F, Gas 4) and bake the pastry case empty for a further 5–7 minutes or until the bottom is crisp and lightly golden.

TREACLE TART

INGREDIENTS

Makes a 20.5cm (8in) tart, to serve 6
ROUGH PUFF PASTRY:

140g (5oz) plain flour

a large pinch of salt

35g (1¼oz) butter, chilled and diced

35g (1¼oz) lard or white vegetable fat, chilled and diced

2–3 tablespoons icy water to bind

FILLING:

about 6 rounded tablespoons golden syrup (see recipe)

about 110g (4oz) fresh white breadcrumbs

the grated rind and juice of 1 large unwaxed lemon, or to taste

a 20.5cm (8in) loose-based flan tin

ARRANGE THE PASTRY STRIPS ON THE FILLING TO MAKE A NEAT WOVEN LATTICE.

This is an old-fashioned nursery pudding that is always very popular. The recipe here has plenty of lemon to flavour the filling of golden syrup and breadcrumbs. I like to use rough puff pastry for the tart case, but you can also use a simple shortcrust (see page 133) or a slightly sweet rich shortcrust (see the recipe for Lemon Meringue Pie on page 156).

To make the rough puff pastry, sift the flour and salt into a mixing bowl. Add the cold diced fats and stir gently with a round-bladed knife until they are coated with flour. Stir in just enough icy water to bind the dough – it should be very lumpy and soft but not sticky or wet.

Turn the dough on to a lightly floured work surface and form it into a brick shape. Using a floured rolling pin, roll out the dough away from you into a rectangle about 1cm (³⁄₈in) thick. Fold the dough in three like a business letter: fold the bottom third of the dough up to cover the centre third, then fold the top third down to cover the other two layers. Gently but firmly seal the edges by pressing down with the rolling pin. This is the first 'turn'. Lift up the piece of dough and give it a quarter turn anti-clockwise, so that the folded edges are now at the sides. Roll out and fold in three again, just as before, then give the dough a quarter turn anti-clockwise; repeat. After this third 'turn', wrap the dough and chill for 20 minutes, then do three more 'turns' – to make a total of six. Chill for 20 minutes.

Roll out the dough to a round about 25.5cm (10in) in diameter and use to line the tin. Roll the pin over the top of the tin to cut off the excess dough. Reserve the trimmings to make the lattice. Chill the pastry case and trimmings while you make the filling.

Preheat the oven to 200C (400F, Gas 6).

Gently heat the syrup until it becomes runny, then remove from the heat and stir in the breadcrumbs and lemon rind and juice. Leave to stand for 10 minutes. If the mixture seems very sloppy, add another spoonful of crumbs; if the mixture seems stiff and dry, add another spoonful of syrup.

Treacle Tart (left), Croustade aux Pommes (see recipe on page 176).

Taste the mixture and add more lemon juice if necessary.

Spoon the filling into the pastry case; don't press down to level the surface. Roll out the dough trimmings 6mm (¼in) thick and cut into thin strips. Lay the strips across the filling to make a lattice pattern, sticking the ends to the rim of the pastry case with a little cold water. The pastry strips can be twisted before sticking the ends down if you want to make the tart look fancier.

Bake for 15 minutes, then reduce the oven temperature to 190C (375F, Gas 5) and bake for a further 10 minutes or until golden. Serve warm.

LEMON TART

INGREDIENTS

Makes a 23cm (9in) tart, to serve 6
PASTRY:
140g (5oz) plain flour
a pinch of salt
85g (3oz) unsalted butter, chilled and diced
30g (1oz) caster sugar
1 egg yolk
1–2 tablespoons icy water
a little egg white, lightly beaten, for brushing

FILLING:
3 eggs
1 egg yolk
140ml (5fl oz) double cream
110g (4oz) caster sugar
the grated rind of 2 unwaxed lemons
the juice of 3 lemons

a 23cm (9in) loose-based flan tin
a baking tray

In a weekend newspaper, I once read a review of fashionable restaurants rated according to the quality of the lemon tarts they served! It is hard to get the balance right when making this dessert — the pastry must be crisp, and the filling should be lemony, creamy, fresh-tasting and fairly light. In the simple recipe here, the filling is like a light lemon curd made with cream rather than butter. Serve the tart with fresh strawberries or raspberries, and crème fraîche. Use unwaxed lemons if possible; otherwise scrub the fruit well with hot soapy water before grating the rind.

To make the pastry dough, sift the flour and salt into a bowl, add the diced butter and rub into the flour, using the tips of your fingers, until the mixture resembles fine crumbs. Stir in the sugar. Add the egg yolk and 1 tablespoon of water and stir into the flour mixture to bind, using a round-bladed knife; add more water if necessary. Quickly bring the mixture together with your hands, without kneading, to make a firm but not sticky ball of dough. Alternatively, you can make the dough in a food processor (see page 132). Wrap the dough and chill for about 30 minutes.

Roll out the dough on a lightly floured work surface to a round about 28cm (11in) in diameter and use to line the flan tin. Trim off the excess dough by rolling the pin across the top of the tin, then neaten the rim. Prick the bottom of the pastry case with a fork, then chill for 15 minutes.

Preheat the oven to 190C (375F, Gas 5).

Bake the pastry case blind (see page 158). It is important to cook the pastry thoroughly or the base of the finished tart will be soggy. Remove from the oven but do not unmould. Immediately brush the bottom of the pastry case with a little egg white, and leave to cool. (The egg white helps to keep the pastry from turning soggy once the filling is added.) Reduce the oven temperature to 170C (325F, Gas 3) and put a baking tray in the oven to heat up.

To make the filling, put all the ingredients into a large jug and whisk, by hand, just until thoroughly combined.

Set the pastry case, still in the tin, on the hot baking tray and pour in three-quarters of the filling. Put into the oven, then carefully pour in the rest of the filling – this way you avoid spilling the filling as you put the tart into the oven. Bake for 25–30 minutes or until the filling is firm when the tart is gently shaken. Leave to cool before unmoulding. Serve at room temperature or chilled.

RIGHT The display of luscious tarts at La Boîte à Dessert in Lyons.

STRAWBERRY CHEESE TART

This light summery dessert, a cross between a cheesecake and a creamy fruit flan, comes from Rosemary Underdahl of Yarmouth, Maine (see pages 18-19 for her wonderful cookie recipes). She says that out of season the strawberries can be replaced with pears lightly poached in — leftover — sparkling wine or champagne, rosé for choice, or with sliced nectarines. The pastry for the tart is very rich so it is best rolled out between sheets of cling film or baking parchment.

To make the pastry, mix the flour with the sugar and salt, then rub in the butter, using your fingertips, until the mixture resembles fine crumbs. Add 2 tablespoons orange juice and stir into the flour mixture to bind, using a round-bladed knife; add more orange juice if necessary. Quickly bring the mixture together with your hands, without kneading, to make a fairly firm dough that is not dry or crumbly. Alternatively, you can make the dough in a food processor (see page 132). Shape the dough into a flat disc, then wrap and chill for 10 minutes.

Roll out the dough between two sheets of cling film or non-stick baking parchment to a round about 30.5cm (12in) in diameter. Peel off the top sheet of film or paper, turn the round of dough over and lay it over the tin. Gently press the dough into the tin to line the bottom and sides evenly, then peel off the remaining cling film or paper. Do not cut off the excess pastry dough, but instead fold it back into the tin and press gently, to make the sides twice as thick. Prick the bottom of the pastry case all over with a fork, then cover and chill in the freezer for 30 minutes.

INGREDIENTS

Makes a 25.5cm (10in) tart, to serve 8
PASTRY:
210g (7¹/₂oz) plain flour
1 tablespoon caster sugar
a pinch of salt
110g (4oz) unsalted butter, chilled and diced
2–3 tablespoons orange juice to bind

FILLING:
340g (12oz) cream cheese — Philadelphia brand
  seems to work best
100g (3¹/₂oz) caster sugar
2 eggs, size 2, beaten
1 tablespoon grated orange rind
150g (about 5oz) strawberries, thinly sliced

GLAZE:
3 tablespoons apricot or strawberry conserve
1 tablespoon lemon juice

a 25.5cm (10in) loose-based flan tin

Preheat the oven to 200C (400F, Gas 6).

Line the chilled pastry case with non-stick baking parchment and fill with baking beans (see the instructions for baking blind on page 158). Bake for about 10 minutes or until just firm, then remove the paper and beans and bake for a further 8–10 minutes or until lightly browned. Leave the pastry case to cool completely.

Lower the oven temperature to 180C (350F, Gas 4).

To make the filling, beat the cream cheese with the sugar until smooth and creamy, then gradually beat in the eggs followed by the orange rind.

Pour the filling into the cold pastry case. Bake for 30 minutes or until set. Leave to cool on a wire rack before unmoulding.

Arrange the sliced strawberries on top. To make the glaze, heat the conserve with the lemon juice until runny, then sieve into a clean pan. Warm gently and then brush over the fruit to glaze it lightly. Chill for about 1 hour before serving.

Strawberries in the market at Lyons.

STRAWBERRY MARZIPAN TART

I am very fond of the combination of strawberries and almonds, which makes this a favourite dessert. It is quite a substantial tart – the pastry case is filled with an almond sponge flavoured with orange and then topped with sliced fruit. For a glossy finish the arranged strawberries can be brushed with a glaze of hot redcurrant jelly, but if the fruit is loaded with flavour I prefer to leave it plain. As with most almond desserts, this tart improves on keeping a day or so before the fruit is added.

To make the pastry dough, sift the flour into a bowl, add the diced butter and rub into the flour, using the tips of your fingers, until the mixture resembles fine crumbs. Stir in the sugar. Add the egg yolk and water and stir into the flour mixture to bind, using a round-bladed knife; add more water if necessary. Quickly bring the mixture together with your hands, without kneading, to make a soft but not sticky ball of dough. Alternatively, you can make the dough in a food processor (see page 132). Wrap the dough and chill for 20 minutes.

Preheat the oven to 180C (350F, Gas 4).

Roll out the pastry dough on a lightly floured work surface to a round about 28cm (11in) in diameter and use to line the flan tin. Chill while preparing the filling.

Beat the butter until creamy, then beat in the sugar and continue beating until light and fluffy. Gradually beat in the eggs, beating well after each addition. Beat in the orange rind and juice, then fold in the ground almonds using a large metal spoon. Spoon the filling into the pastry case and level the surface.

Bake in the preheated oven for 45 minutes to 1 hour or until golden and firm to the touch. Leave to cool before unmoulding. If possible, wrap the tart and store in an airtight tin overnight before finishing.

Arrange the sliced strawberries in overlapping circles on top of the tart just before serving. Serve at room temperature.

INGREDIENTS

Makes a 23cm (9in) tart, to serve 6–8
PASTRY:
170g (6oz) plain flour
100g (3½oz) unsalted butter, chilled and diced
30g (1oz) caster sugar
1 egg yolk
about 1 tablespoon icy water

FILLING:
230g (8oz) unsalted butter, at room temperature
85g (3oz) caster sugar
2 eggs, beaten
the grated rind and juice of 1 unwaxed orange
230g (8oz) ground almonds

TOPPING:
230g (8oz) ripe strawberries, hulled and sliced

a 23cm (9in) loose-based flan tin

TARTE TATIN

Makes a 30.5cm (12in) tart, to serve
   8–10
PASTRY:
200g (7oz) plain flour
a pinch of salt
30g (1oz) caster sugar
100g (3½oz) unsalted butter, chilled and diced
1 egg yolk
2 tablespoons icy water

FILLING:
110g (4oz) unsalted butter
200g (7oz) caster sugar
about 2kg (4lb 6oz) dessert apples, such as Cox's
   Orange Pippin, Granny Smith, Golden
   Delicious, Egremont Russet

a 30.5cm (12in) heavy frying pan or skillet with
   an ovenproof handle, or a tarte tatin tin

This upside-down apple tart, traditionally cooked in a heavy cast-iron frying pan, can be made with puff pastry or a sweet shortcrust. I find the classic French recipe slightly too rich, heavy and sweet to enjoy at the end of a meal, so mine uses less butter and sugar. Here you can really taste the fruit as well as the caramel. It is best to use tart eating apples for the filling – cooking apples release too much liquid – and to pack them together tightly. Do not put the pastry on top of the apples until they are sitting in a good brown caramel or the tart will be soggy and insipid-tasting.

Make the pastry dough by hand (see page 132) or in a food processor: put the flour, salt and sugar in the bowl of the processor and process until mixed. Add the diced butter and process until the mixture resembles fine crumbs. With the machine running, add the egg yolk and icy water through the feed tube, and process until the mixture binds together to form a firm but not dry dough. If there are dry crumbs, gradually add a little more water. Wrap and chill while preparing the apples.

1 COOK THE APPLE HALVES IN THE FRYING PAN WITH THE BUTTER AND SUGAR UNTIL A RICH CARAMEL IS FORMED AND MOISTURE FROM THE APPLES HAS EVAPORATED.

2 COVER THE CARAMELISED APPLES WITH THE PASTRY LID, GENTLY UNROLLING IT FROM THE ROLLING PIN, THEN TUCK THE EDGES DOWN INSIDE THE PAN.

Cut the butter into thin slices and arrange on the bottom of the frying pan to cover completely. Sprinkle over the sugar to make an even layer. Peel, halve and core the apples. Arrange in the pan, on top of the butter and sugar, so the apple halves stand up vertically. Pack the apples tightly together so the tart will not collapse in the oven.

Put the pan over a moderate heat on top of the stove and cook for 20–30 minutes or until the butter and sugar have formed a richly coloured caramel, and all the moisture from the apples has evaporated. Remove from the heat.

While the apples are cooking, preheat the oven to 220C (425F, Gas 7).

Roll out the dough on a lightly floured surface to a round to fit the top of the pan. Roll up the dough around the rolling pin and lift over the pan. Gently unroll the dough so it covers the apples completely. Quickly tuck the edges of the dough down inside the pan, then prick the pastry lid all over with a fork. Bake for 20–30 minutes or until golden brown and crisp.

Cool slightly, then loosen the pastry edges and turn out the tart upside down so the pastry is under the caramelised apples. Eat warm or at room temperature, with ice-cream, crème fraîche or fromage frais.

SUMMER FRUIT TART

This pretty, fresh fruit tart comes from Katie Barber, who has recently moved from Wymondham, where she ran a successful restaurant, to central France. There she has opened her house to bed-and-breakfast guests, and has gained a reputation among the local population for cooking very good dinners.

INGREDIENTS

Makes a 23–25.5cm (9–10in) tart, to
    serve 8

½ batch puff pastry dough (page 144), about
    300g (10½oz)

2 tablespoons liqueur de noisette, eau de vie or
    kirsch

2–3 large, ripe peaches

about 12 ripe apricots

230g (8oz) ripe dessert cherries

3 tablespoons redcurrant jelly

1 tablespoon toasted flaked almonds

blackcurrant leaves to decorate (optional)

PASTRY CREAM:

280ml (10fl oz) rich creamy milk

1 vanilla pod, split, or 1 teaspoon pure vanilla
    essence

4 egg yolks, size 2

60g (2oz) caster sugar or vanilla sugar

2 tablespoons plain flour

a 23–25.5cm (9–10in) loose-based flan tin

ABOVE Katie Barber proudly shows off her Summer Fruit Tart.

OPPOSITE Juicy, aromatic summer fruits being prepared for sale in the market at Lyons.

Preheat the oven to 200C (400F, Gas 6).

On a floured work surface, roll out the pastry dough to a round about 6.5cm (2½in) larger than your flan tin. Use the dough to line the tin, letting the excess dough drape over the rim. Chill for 15 minutes, then cut off the excess dough with a very sharp knife, taking care not to stretch it. Prick the bottom of the pastry case all over with a fork, then bake blind (see page 158). Leave until completely cold. (It is important to cook the pastry case well or the tart will become soggy soon after assembling.)

To make the pastry cream, put the milk and the split vanilla pod (but not the essence) into a heavy saucepan and heat slowly until scalding hot. Remove from the heat, cover the pan and leave to infuse for 20 minutes. Whisk the egg yolks with the sugar until very light and thick, then whisk in the flour until there are no lumps. Remove the vanilla pod, then whisk the milk into the egg mixture. Tip the mixture into the saucepan and cook over moderate heat, whisking constantly, until the mixture boils and thickens to a smooth creamy consistency. Cook gently, whisking, for a couple of minutes or until there is no raw flour taste. Remove from the heat and stir in the vanilla essence, if using. Sprinkle the top of the pastry cream with a little sugar or melted butter to prevent a skin from forming, then leave to cool.

Add half the liqueur to the cold pastry cream and beat until completely smooth. Spread over the bottom of the cold pastry case.

Prepare the fruit: slice the peaches; halve or quarter the apricots; stone the cherries, leaving a few whole and joined by the stalks in pairs for decoration. Arrange the fruit attractively over the pastry cream.

Heat the redcurrant jelly with the rest of the liqueur and stir vigorously until smooth, then brush over the fruit to glaze it. Scatter over the almonds and serve as soon as possible, decorated with blackcurrant leaves and the reserved cherries.

NOTE To make a lighter pastry cream, you can stir in 140ml (5fl oz) cream which has been lightly whipped just before it is to be used.

VARIATIONS: MIXED FRUIT TART Make the pastry case and pastry cream as above, but omitting the liqueur. Decorate with small whole fruits, such as tiny apricots and figs, grapes, cherries, strawberries, redcurrants, raspberries and Fantasia dessert blackberries, plus tiny vine leaves and wild roses. Let your imagination run riot.

APRICOT TART Make the pastry case and pastry cream as above, but omitting the liqueur. Add 1 tablespoon each of ground almonds, almond or apricot liqueur and whipped cream to the pastry cream. Decorate with poached apricot halves and flaked almonds, and glaze with the apricot poaching liquid, well reduced, or apricot jelly.

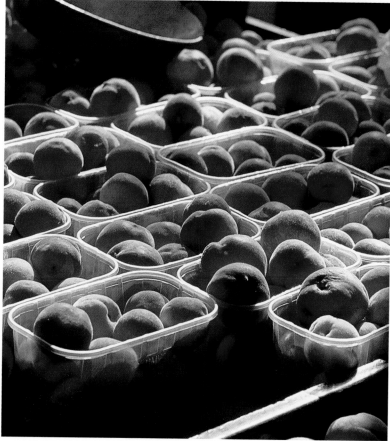

TARTE À LA CRÈME

Makes a 27.5cm (10³/₄in) tart, to serve 8–10

¹/₂ batch puff pastry dough (page 144), about 300g (10¹/₂oz)

1 litre (1³/₄ pints) UHT French cream (see note)

80g (3oz) caster sugar

a 27.5cm (10³/₄in) loose-based flan tin

NOTE: The only cream that works is UHT long-life French cream. It is available from larger supermarkets and delis and by mail order from Vivian's, 2 Worple Way, Richmond, Surrey TW10 6DF (tel: 0181 940 3600).

This recipe comes from restaurateurs Max Renzland and his twin brother, the late Marc Renzland, whose friendliness and skills as a chef are sadly missed. Their first restaurant, in Kew in Surrey, quickly gained a reputation for some of the best, and most scrupulously French, food in London. Their hospitality overwhelmed their customers...and eventually their restaurant because portions were more than generous, extra courses were added at no extra charge, and wine was used in sauces by the magnum rather than by the ladle. The restaurant closed, but a while later they turned up further down the Thames, cooking at a café restaurant, Le Petit Max, in Hampton Wick. There is now also a larger place in London, Chez Max in Ifield Road. This tart has been on every one of their menus since they first opened. A combination of light, buttery pastry and pure cream, it is wonderful.

Roll out the pastry dough to a large, thin round about 35cm (13³/₄in) in diameter and use to line the flan tin. Let the excess dough hang over the edge of the tin – do not cut it off. Chill for 25 minutes.

Preheat the oven to 200C (400F, Gas 6).

Prick the bottom of the pastry case all over with a fork, then bake until crisp and golden, about 15 minutes. Leave to cool in the tin.

Put the cream and sugar in a heavy-based saucepan and slowly bring to the boil. Simmer until reduced by 60% – about 1 hour – stirring frequently. Pour into the baked tart case and carefully slide into the oven (at the same temperature). Bake for about 15 minutes or until golden. Leave to cool, then use a sharp knife to trim off the excess pastry. Serve at room temperature.

CAREFULLY POUR THE HOT, THICKENED CREAM INTO THE BAKED PASTRY CASE.

RIGHT Marc Renzland with a Tarte à la Crème – the pastry edges are trimmed after baking and cooling.

DANISH STRAWBERRY SHORTBREAD

INGREDIENTS

Serves 6–8
SHORTBREAD BASE:
230g (8oz) plain flour
a pinch of salt
70g (2½oz) icing sugar
170g (6oz) unsalted butter, chilled and diced
2 egg yolks, size 2
a few drops of pure vanilla essence

TOPPING:
450g (1lb) ripe strawberries, hulled
about 230g (8oz) seedless raspberry or redcurrant
  jelly
1–2 tablespoons water

a large baking tray, greased

This gorgeous summer dessert, of rich, crisp shortbread topped with whole strawberries under a shiny glaze, is adapted from a Cordon Bleu recipe. With a food processor the base is so simple to make, and you can use any soft fruit in season — raspberries, the large sweet Fantasia dessert blackberries, peaches, apricots — with a suitable jelly or sieved jam to glaze.

Above SHAPE, FLUTE AND PRICK THE PASTRY BASE, THEN CHILL IT WELL BEFORE BAKING.

Top right BRUSH THE JELLY GLAZE OVER THE STRAWBERRIES. FOR AN EVEN, THIN COVERING THE JELLY GLAZE MUST BE BOILING HOT.

To make the shortbread, sift the flour, salt and icing sugar into the bowl of the food processor. Add the diced butter and process until the mixture resembles fine crumbs. With the machine running, add the yolks and vanilla essence through the feed tube. When the mixture has come together, remove it, shape into a ball and wrap. Chill until the dough is firm enough to roll out — about 30 minutes.

Roll out the dough on the prepared baking tray to a round about 25.5cm (10in) in diameter and about 6mm (¼in) thick. Flute the edge by pinching the dough between your fingers, then prick the base all over with a fork. Chill for about 10 minutes.

Preheat the oven to 180C (350F, Gas 4).

Bake the shortbread base for 20–25 minutes or until just firm and lightly golden. Leave on the baking tray until cool and quite firm before attempting to transfer to a wire rack. When the shortbread base is cold, place it on a serving platter or bread board.

To prepare the topping, check the strawberries for blemishes, then wipe gently to clean them — wash only if the berries look gritty or muddy or you are dubious about them. Put the jelly into a small saucepan with 1 tablespoon of water. Heat gently, stirring frequently as the jelly melts, then beat vigorously with a wooden spoon to make a smooth, thick syrup.

Brush a little hot jelly over the shortbread base. Arrange the strawberries upright on the base with the pointed ends upwards — I find it easiest to start at the edge. The berries should cover the shortbread base completely. Brush the berries with the boiling hot jelly glaze to coat them thoroughly. If the glaze becomes thick and difficult to use, reheat it and add a little extra water. Leave to set — about 20 minutes — then serve with cream or ice-cream. Eat within about 4 hours of assembling.

PLUM TART

INGREDIENTS

Makes a 20.5cm (8in) tart, to serve 6
PASTRY:
70g (2¹/₂oz) unsalted butter, at room temperature
40g (1¹/₂oz) icing sugar, sifted
the grated rind of ¹/₂ unwaxed lemon
1 egg yolk
140g (5oz) plain flour

FILLING:
10 ripe plums, about 500g (1lb 2oz)
2 tablespoons ground almonds
30g (1oz) unsalted butter, cut into small pieces
2 tablespoons caster or demerara sugar, or to taste, for sprinkling
30g (1oz) slivered almonds

a 20.5cm (8in) cast-iron frying pan or skillet or a loose-based flan tin

This recipe is based on a tart I enjoyed in Düsseldorf. It arrived at the table in a small cast-iron pan, and tasted as wonderful as it looked. Fully ripe purple plums that are juicy and sweet are the best to use; you can also use yellow plums or greengages, although you may have to add extra sugar. The tart can also be made in a loose-based flan tin.

To make the pastry, beat the butter until creamy, then beat in the sugar and lemon rind. When the mixture is light and fluffy, beat in the egg yolk. Work in the flour, first stirring and then gently kneading to bring the dough together. It should be soft but not sticky. Wrap and chill until firm – about 1 hour.

Roll out the dough on a lightly floured surface to a round about 25.5cm (10in) in diameter and use to line the pan or flan tin. (If using a pan, it is easiest to cut out a neat round of dough for lining.) Prick the bottom of the pastry case all over with a fork, then chill for 20 minutes.

Meanwhile, rinse and quarter the plums, discarding the stones. Preheat the oven to 190C (375F, Gas 5).

Sprinkle the ground almonds over the bottom of the pastry case. Arrange the plum quarters on top so the fleshy side is uppermost. Dot with the butter and sprinkle with the sugar. Bake for 30 minutes or until the fruit is almost tender. Scatter over the almonds and bake for a few more minutes or until the almonds are golden. Serve warm or at room temperature.

1 PUT THE ROUND OF DOUGH IN THE PAN AND PRESS ON TO THE BOTTOM AND SIDES TO REMOVE ANY AIR BUBBLES.

2 SPRINKLE IN THE GROUND ALMONDS. THEY WILL ABSORB THE PLUM JUICE AND PREVENT THE PASTRY BECOMING SOGGY.

3 ARRANGE THE PLUM QUARTERS ON THE LAYER OF GROUND ALMONDS, WITH THE SKIN SIDE UNDERNEATH.

4 DOT THE PLUMS WITH SMALL PIECES OF BUTTER AND SPRINKLE WITH SUGAR TO GIVE A MOIST TOPPING.

ENGLISH DEEP FRUIT PIE

Makes a medium pie, to serve 6
PASTRY:
170g (6oz) plain flour
110g (4oz) unsalted butter, chilled and diced
about 4 tablespoons icy water

FILLING:
about 1.1kg (2½lb) apples (see right)
about 3 tablespoons light muscovado sugar, to taste
2 tablespoons water or orange or lemon juice
sugar for sprinkling

a deep pie dish, about 22 x 16cm (8¾ x 6¼in)

The traditional English fruit pie is made in a special oval china or ovenproof glass dish, deep enough for plenty of filling. Apples — either Bramleys or a combination of varieties (Bramleys and Cox's tossed with grated orange or lemon rind and juice works well) — make the most popular filling. For variety, they can be flavoured with cinnamon and dark muscovado sugar, or mixed with raisins or sultanas or toasted nuts. Other fruits can be mixed with the apples: blackberries, of course, but also cranberries — fresh, frozen or dried — or fresh or frozen blueberries. Another excellent combination is pear and raspberry. I also like rhubarb (or gooseberries) with sliced oranges, or rhubarb and redcurrants. The pastry, a top crust only, is usually shortcrust, though rough puff makes an excellent covering for cherry or rhubarb pies.

Preheat the oven to 200C (400F, Gas 6).

Make the pastry dough by hand (see page 132) or in a food processor: put the flour and butter into the bowl of the processor and process until the mixture looks like fine crumbs. With the machine running, gradually add the water through the feed tube, to make a soft but not sticky dough. Wrap and chill while preparing the fruit.

Peel, core and thickly slice the apples. Toss them with the sugar and water or juice. Add spices, grated orange or lemon rind or dried fruit to taste and mix well.

Pile the fruit into the pie dish, mounding it slightly in the centre. Some cooks like to use a china pie raiser, putting it in the centre of the dish so the top sticks up above the fruit filling. A pie raiser is good if you are short of filling because it prevents the crust sagging in the middle. Also, if the filling is likely to become very juicy during cooking, the pie raiser will prevent the crust becoming soggy.

Roll out the dough on a floured work surface to an oval about 7.5cm (3in) larger all around than the dish. Cut off a strip of dough about 1cm (³⁄₈in) wide and long enough to fit around the rim of the dish. Dampen the rim of the dish and press the strip of dough on to the rim, joining the ends neatly. Dampen this pastry rim. Lay the remaining piece of dough over the dish, so it completely covers the pie. Press the dough on to the pastry rim to seal the lid to the dish. Trim off the excess dough with a knife — the trimmings can be kept for decorations.

The sides of the crust can be 'knocked up' to give a good-looking edge as well as sealing them: use the back of a small knife held horizontally to make small knocks, or cuts, into the side of the crust all around. The edge

1 PRESS A STRIP OF PASTRY ON TO THE DAMPENED RIM OF THE DISH TO HELP THE CRUST STAY IN PLACE.

2 TO AVOID STRETCHING THE DOUGH, USE THE ROLLING PIN TO SUPPORT IT AS YOU LIFT IT OVER THE PIE.

3 AFTER 'KNOCKING UP' THE SIDE OF THE CRUST, GIVE THE EDGE AN ATTRACTIVE SCALLOPED FINISH.

Apple and Raspberry Pie.

can then be fluted by placing two fingertips on the pastry rim and gently drawing a small knife between them to give a scalloped look. If decorating the crust with dough trimmings, cut out the shapes and stick them on with a little water.

Make a steam hole in the centre of the pie with the tip of a knife or a skewer (directly over the pie raiser, if using), then bake for about 30 minutes or until the pastry is golden and crisp. Sprinkle with sugar, and serve hot, warm or at room temperature.

VARIATIONS If you would rather use rough puff pastry, follow the recipe given on page 141, using 170g (6oz) plain flour and 40g (1¹/₂oz) each butter and lard or white vegetable fat.

If using another fruit with the apples (or pears), use about 900g (2lb) apples plus about 230g (8oz) blackberries, blueberries, cranberries or raspberries, and toss with the water and sugar to taste.

MRS BUSH'S PRIZE-WINNING PIE

Makes a 23cm (9in) pie, to serve 6
FILLING:
2 large Bramley apples, about 450g (1lb)
1 tablespoon water
sugar to taste

PASTRY:
230g (8oz) plain flour
60g (2oz) hard lard, chilled and diced
60g (2oz) salted butter, chilled and diced
8 teaspoons icy water
1 egg, beaten with a pinch of salt, for glazing
1 tablespoon caster sugar for sprinkling

a 23cm (9in) pie plate, about 2cm (³/₄in) deep

RIGHT Mrs Jean Bush with her prize-winning
apple pie. As she says, this pie served with fresh
cream is the true taste of Nottinghamshire.

In the 1994 Open Apple Pie Competition, organised by the Women's Institute in Nottinghamshire, Jean Bush won first prize with this lovely recipe. The competition was held near where the first Bramley apple tree was grown. Hundreds of pies, all made with Bramley apples, were entered.

Meeting Mrs Bush proved difficult as she works long hours as a councillor and a magistrate. But the advice she gave me about baking apple pie was well worth the effort. She cooks the apples first and then leaves them to cool before putting them into the pie. Bramleys make a good pie filling because they have three times more malic acid than Golden Delicious, and nearly twice as much as Cox's Orange Pippins. It is this, and a lower sugar content, that gives them their tangy flavour, which isn't lost during cooking. The unique texture of the Bramley is caused by air trapped in the cells of the apples; this helps the flesh turn wonderfully fluffy as the cells expand with heat.

JEAN BUSH USES A CARDBOARD TEMPLATE
TO CUT PERFECT PASTRY DECORATIONS
FOR HER PIE.

AFTER PUTTING THEM IN PLACE, SHE
BRUSHES THE PIE VERY EVENLY AND
LIGHTLY WITH EGG BEFORE BAKING

Peel, core and slice the apples. Put into a microwave-proof dish with the tablespoon of water and cook in the microwave on high setting for 2 minutes. Leave to cool, then add sugar to taste.

While the apples are cooling, make the pastry dough. Sift the flour into a large mixing bowl, add the fats and cut into very small pieces, then rub into the flour, using your fingertips, until the mixture resembles fine crumbs. Add the water and toss with a round-bladed knife to bind the ingredients. Knead lightly to make a soft but not sticky dough, then wrap and chill for 20 minutes, if necessary.

Preheat the oven to 220C (425F, Gas 7).

Roll out half of the pastry dough on a cold, floured work surface to a round about 30.5cm (12in) in diameter. Use to line the pie dish, leaving the excess dough hanging over the edge. Spoon in the apple filling. Roll out the rest of the pastry dough to a round as before. Brush the rim of the pie case with water, then cover the pie with the pastry lid. Press the edges together to seal, then trim off the excess dough and flute the edges with a fork. This makes the pie look attractive as well as helping to seal together the pastry case and lid.

Gather up the dough trimmings, knead them together lightly and then roll out thinly. Cut out decorations such as leaves, apples or an apple tree. Stick the decorations to the pie with a little water, then brush the top of the pie all over with the beaten egg. Cut a slit in the middle of the lid.

Bake in the preheated oven for 30 minutes or until golden and crisp. Sprinkle with sugar, and serve hot, warm or at room temperature.

BELOW Judges Wendy Whittaker and Duncan Goodhew examine the entries in the 1994 Open Apple Pie Competition. The judging took several hours.

BELOW RIGHT Judge Margaret Foss takes a closer look at one of the entries.

CROUSTADE AUX POMMES

INGREDIENTS

Makes a 30.5cm (12in) pie, to serve 8
250g (8³/₄oz) phyllo pastry (see recipe)
140g (5oz) unsalted butter
4 Bramley apples, about 900g (2lb)
110g (4oz) caster sugar
1–2 tablespoons Calvados (optional)
icing sugar for sprinkling

a 30.5cm (12in) springclip tin, greased and
  sprinkled with sugar

The beauty of this apple pie, from the south-west of France, is its simplicity: there is no pastry to make, just sheets of phyllo to butter and arrange in the tin. The filling is simply Bramley apples cooked in butter and sugar until golden and slightly caramelised. The best tin to use is a springclip, although you could also use a deep flan tin, taking care not to let the pastry stick to the rim.

If the pastry is frozen, thaw according to the packet instructions. Once unwrapped, keep the pastry covered with cling film or a damp tea towel to prevent it from drying out.

Melt 60g (2oz) of the butter in a large heavy pan. Peel, core and thickly slice the apples, then put into the hot butter and cook until almost tender. The slices should keep their shape as much as possible, so don't stir, but shake the pan from time to time to prevent them from sticking. Sprinkle over 60g (2oz) of the sugar and cook, tossing and shaking the pan, until the sugar starts to caramelise the apples. Remove from the heat, sprinkle with the Calvados and leave to cool.

Preheat the oven to 220C (425F, Gas 7).

1 LINE THE TIN WITH OVERLAPPING SHEETS OF PHYLLO, BRUSHING THEM WITH BUTTER AND SPRINKLING WITH SUGAR.

2 SPOON THE COOLED CARAMELISED APPLE AND CALVADOS FILLING INTO THE PHYLLO-LINED TIN.

3 FOLD IN THE EDGES OF THE PASTRY TO COVER THE FILLING, THEN BRUSH WITH BUTTER AND SPRINKLE WITH SUGAR.

4 GENTLY ARRANGE THE CRUMPLED SHEETS OF PHYLLO PASTRY ON THE TOP, PILING THEM UP.

DUST THE WARM CROUSTADE WITH ICING SUGAR BEFORE SERVING.

Melt the rest of the butter in a small pan. Line the bottom of the prepared tin with two or three sheets of phyllo pastry, overlapping them where necessary and letting the edges flop over the rim of the tin. Brush the layered pastry with a little melted butter and sprinkle with some of the remaining sugar. Add another two or three sheets of phyllo; brush with butter and sprinkle with sugar. Repeat once more so that about half the phyllo has been used. Spoon in the apple filling, then fold the edges of the phyllo in over the filling as if wrapping a parcel. Brush the folded-in pieces of phyllo with butter and sprinkle with sugar. Lightly brush the remaining sheets of phyllo with butter, then cut or tear them in half, across or diagonally. Crumple up each piece, rather like a chiffon scarf, and gently arrange in a pile on top of the apples – the whole thing should resemble a big, silly, frilly hat.

Sprinkle with any remaining butter, then bake for about 20 minutes or until golden and crisp. Carefully unmould and dust liberally with sifted icing sugar. Serve warm, with ice-cream or crème fraîche, or an apple and Calvados sorbet.

DOUBLE CRUST FRUIT PIES

YOU CAN SEAL THE PASTRY RIM BY CRIMPING WITH THE BACK OF A FORK.

As in the English Deep Fruit Pie on page 172, the fruit and the pastry in the double crust fruit pies here can be varied to suit the season and your fancy. A metal pie plate will give the crispest pastry base because it conducts heat the best, although ovenproof glass and china pie plates can also be used. It is best to bake these pies on a baking tray to catch any juices that bubble out. Some cooks like to toss very juicy fruit – peaches and cherries, for example – with a little cornflour so the filling will hold together instead of running out when the pie is cut. You can make a plain closed top crust or a lattice top (see below). For a plain top crust, roll out the larger portion of dough into a round 2.5cm (1in) larger than the diameter of the pie plate and use to cover the pie. Firmly press the top crust on to the dampened border of the bottom crust to seal, then cut off the excess dough with a sharp knife. 'Knock up' the sides (see page 172), then finish the edge by crimping – pressing down with the back of a fork – or fluting with your fingers. Make a steam hole in the centre of the top crust and decorate, if wished, with leaves cut from the dough trimmings.

RHUBARB AND ORANGE PIE

Both shortcrust and rough puff pastry are suitable for this irresistible pie. When redcurrants are in season, use them instead of orange, as an unusual companion for the rhubarb.

INGREDIENTS

Makes a 23cm (9in) pie, to serve 6
PASTRY:
280g (10oz) plain flour
a pinch of salt
70g (2¹/₂oz) unsalted butter, chilled and diced
70g (2¹/₂oz) lard or white vegetable fat, chilled and diced
1 tablespoon caster sugar plus more for sprinkling
about 4 tablespoons icy water to bind

FILLING:
680g (1¹/₂lb) trimmed young rhubarb
1 unwaxed orange
about 4 tablespoons sugar, to taste

a 23cm (9in) pie plate, about 2cm (³/₄in) deep
a baking tray

Preheat the oven to 200C (400F, Gas 6).

To make the pastry dough, sift the flour and salt into a bowl, add the diced fat and rub into the flour, using the tips of your fingers, until the mixture resembles fine crumbs. Stir in the sugar. Add 3 tablespoons of water and stir into the flour mixture to bind, using a round-bladed knife; add more water if necessary. Quickly bring the mixture together with your hands, without kneading, to make a soft but not sticky ball of dough. Alternatively, you can make the dough in a food processor (see page 132). Wrap the dough and chill while you make the filling.

Wash the rhubarb, then cut into pieces about 2cm (³/₄in) long. Grate the rind from the orange and reserve. Cut off all the peel and white pith, then either slice the orange thinly or cut out segments, depending on the quality of the flesh. Mix the rhubarb with the grated orange rind, orange slices or segments and the sugar.

Divide the dough into two portions, one slightly smaller than the other. Roll out the smaller portion on a lightly floured work surface to a round about 28cm (11in) in diameter and use to line the pie plate, letting the excess dough drape over the rim of the plate. Spoon in the filling, leaving the border around the rim of the plate clear and mounding the fruit neatly in the centre. Brush the pastry border with cold water. Roll out the rest of the dough to a round about 25.5cm (10in) in diameter and stamp out a lattice with a special cutter. Put the lattice top in place and press the edges to seal. (Alternatively, cut strips and arrange them in a lattice pattern as in

OPPOSITE Rhubarb and Orange Pie. The lattice topping on this pie was made using a lattice cutter (available from Lakeland Plastics; see page 190).

the American Blueberry Pie on page 180.) Finish by 'knocking up' and then crimping or fluting the edge (see opposite).

Set the pie plate on a baking tray and bake for 20 minutes. Reduce the oven temperature to 180C (350F, Gas 4) and bake for a further 10–15 minutes or until the pastry is golden. Sprinkle with sugar, and serve warm.

AMERICAN BLUEBERRY PIE

Makes a 23cm (9in) pie, to serve 6
PASTRY:
280g (10oz) plain flour
$^1/_4$ teaspoon salt
$1^3/_4$ tablespoons caster sugar
185g (6$^1/_2$oz) unsalted butter, chilled and diced
3 tablespoons cold milk plus more for glazing

FILLING:
450g (1lb) fresh or frozen blueberries
$^1/_2$ teaspoon ground cinnamon
60g (2oz) plain flour
230g (8oz) caster sugar, or to taste
15g ($^1/_2$oz) butter

a 23cm (9in) pie plate, about 2cm ($^3/_4$in) deep
a baking tray

Wild blueberries taste better than cultivated ones, so look out for them for this luscious pie, even frozen wild berries. The rich pastry, bound with milk rather than the more usual water, is best rolled out between sheets of cling film or paper.

Make the pastry in a food processor: sift the flour, salt and sugar into the processor bowl, add the butter and process until the mixture resembles fine crumbs. With the machine running, add enough milk through the feed tube to make a soft but not sticky dough. Wrap and chill for 30 minutes.

Divide the dough into two portions, one slightly larger than the other. Roll out each portion between two sheets of cling film or non-stick baking parchment to a thin round; the round from the larger portion should be about 28cm (11in) in diameter and that from the smaller portion should be about 24cm (9$^1/_2$in). Chill the smaller round, and use the other to line the pie plate: peel off the top sheet of film or paper, turn the round of dough over and lay it over the pie plate. Gently press the dough into the plate to line the bottom and sides evenly, then peel off the remaining cling film or paper. Do not cut off the excess pastry dough.

To make the filling, mix together all the ingredients except for the butter. Spoon into the pastry-lined pie plate and dot with the butter, cut into small pieces. Brush the pastry rim with a little water. Peel the film or paper from the remaining dough round. Cut into strips about 1cm ($^3/_8$in)

wide and arrange over the filling to make a lattice, sticking the ends of the strips to the pastry rim with a little water. (Alternatively, you can leave the pastry lid plain – see page 178 – but don't make a steam hole in the centre. Trim and seal the edges together firmly, then 'knock up' the sides (see page 172) and flute or crimp the edges neatly.) Chill the pie for 30 minutes.

Preheat the oven to 220C (425F, Gas 7).

Brush the pastry lattice or lid with milk to glaze. If the lid is plain, use a small sharp knife to make eight or nine slits, evenly spaced. Set the pie plate on a baking tray and bake for 25–30 minutes or until the pastry is golden and the filling is bubbling through the lattice or slits. Serve warm, with ice-cream.

SHEILA'S PEACH PIE

INGREDIENTS

Makes a 23cm (9in) pie, to serve 8
PASTRY:
200g (7oz) plain flour
140g (5oz) unsalted butter, chilled and diced
40g (1½oz) ground almonds
40g (1½oz) icing sugar, sifted
1 egg yolk
2 tablespoons cold milk

FILLING:
900g (2lb) peaches
60g (2oz) caster sugar
½ teaspoon ground cinnamon
3 tablespoons cornflour
15g (½oz) ground almonds

TO FINISH:
1 egg white, beaten, for brushing
caster sugar for sprinkling

a 23cm (9in) pie dish, about 4cm (1½in)
   deep, or loose-based flan tin
a baking tray

This recipe comes from an American friend, Dr Sheila Rossan, whom I met every day for years at the local swimming pool. We used to swap recipes, and bring in samples to aid recovery from our exertions. This is her masterpiece – the best peach pie you are ever likely to eat. It has a very rich and delicate pastry that is quite hard to handle and which is best made in a food processor. The filling needs good ripe peaches, and the cornflour helps to thicken the juices released during baking. You can make this in a very deep pie plate or a loose-based flan tin.

Make the pastry dough in a food processor: put the flour and the diced butter into the bowl and process just until the mixture resembles coarse crumbs. Add the ground almonds and sugar and process or pulse briefly just to mix. With the machine running, add the egg yolk and milk through the feed tube and process until the mixture comes together to make a soft but not sticky dough. Wrap and chill for 30 minutes.

Roll out the dough between two pieces of cling film or non-stick baking parchment to a thin round about 30.5cm (12in) in diameter. Peel off the top sheet of film or paper, turn the round of dough over and lay it over the pie dish. Gently press the dough into the dish to line the bottom and sides evenly, then peel off the remaining cling film or paper. If any cracks or tears appear, push the dough together to seal the hole. Trim off the excess dough and keep to make the lattice, then chill the pie case and trimmings while you make the filling.

Preheat the oven to 190C (375F, Gas 5).

Peel the peaches, then slice thickly into a bowl to catch all the juices. Sprinkle over the sugar, cinnamon and cornflour and toss gently to combine. Sprinkle the ground almonds over the bottom of the pie case and spoon the peach mixture on top. Gently knead together the dough trimmings, then roll out thinly and cut into strips about 1cm (³⁄₈in) wide. Arrange over the top of the pie to make a lattice, sticking the ends of the strips to the pastry rim with a little cold water.

Bake the pie for 25 minutes, then brush the pastry lattice with egg white and sprinkle with the sugar. Return to the oven and bake for a further 20–25 minutes or until the pastry is golden and the filling is bubbling. Serve warm, with vanilla ice-cream.

BETTY'S SHOO FLY PIE

INGREDIENTS

Makes a 23cm (9in) pie, to serve 8–10
PASTRY:
185g (6¹/₂oz) plain flour
¹/₄ teaspoon salt
60g (2oz) lard or white vegetable fat, chilled and
    diced
30g (1oz) butter, chilled and diced
2–3 tablespoons icy water

CRUMB TOPPING:
140g (5oz) plain flour
60g (2oz) lard, white vegetable fat or butter,
    chilled and diced
100g (3¹/₂oz) light muscovado sugar

FILLING:
¹/₄ teaspoon salt
1 teaspoon bicarbonate of soda
230ml (8fl oz) boiling water
340g (12oz) golden syrup

a 23cm (9in) pie dish, about 4cm (1¹/₂in) deep,
    or loose-based flan tin

Betty Groff and her favourite Shoo Fly Pie.

While we were in the United States, we were told several times that we had to meet Betty Groff, 'the Julia Child of the Pennsylvania Dutch'. Encouraged by James Beard, she has done more than any other cookery writer to modernise and publicise the food of her community: 'I cook old family dishes with a lighter touch: less cream, butter and stodge. What with central heating, cars and office work, few people want to eat as our grandparents did.' Cooking is in her blood – her grandmother kept a butcher's shop; her father cured hams and air-dried beef; her mother made the pies. It was a strict Mennonite upbringing – Betty had to keep to the dress code – 'but every meal was a party'. The family farmhouse is now a restaurant – called Groff's Farm – and Betty still serves meals family-style. This and the pie on page 184 are her favourite desserts.

Preheat the oven to 190C (375F, Gas 5).

To make the pastry dough, put the flour into a mixing bowl and add the salt and fats. Rub the fat into the flour with the tips of your fingers, or cut it in with a wire pastry cutter, until the mixture resembles fine crumbs. Gradually add enough water just to bind the crumbs together (it will need less on a damp day), tossing the mixture gently with your hand. Press lumps of the dough gently against the sides of the bowl so it comes together. The less the dough is handled, the lighter it will be. Alternatively, you can make the dough in a food processor (see page 132).

Turn the dough on to a generously floured work surface. Gently pat it into a ball, then flatten it lightly and pat the edges to smooth out the rough sides. Roll out the dough into a round about 30.5cm (12in) in diameter and use to line the pie dish. Crimp the edges with your fingers. Put the pastry case into the oven, just as it is, to part-bake for 6–10 minutes; it will just be starting to puff up. (This part-baking helps prevent the pastry from becoming soggy when the filling is added.) Leave to cool while preparing the crumbs and filling.

To make the crumb topping, put all the ingredients into a mixing bowl and rub the fat into the flour and sugar, using your fingertips, until the mixture looks like fine crumbs.

To make the filling, dissolve the salt and bicarbonate of soda in the boiling water in a small saucepan. Then add the golden syrup and mix thoroughly. Bring back to the boil, then remove from the heat and allow to cool slightly.

Pour the filling into the pie case – it should not be more than two-thirds full or the filling will boil over. Sprinkle evenly with the crumb topping. Bake for 10 minutes, then reduce the oven temperature to 180C (350F, Gas 4) and bake for a further 30 minutes or until the centre of the filling doesn't wobble when the pie is shaken. Leave to cool completely, and serve at room temperature.

1 BETTY CRIMPS THE PIE EDGE USING THE THUMB AND FOREFINGER OF ONE HAND AND THE FOREFINGER OF THE OTHER.

2 SHE SPRINKLES THE CRUMB TOPPING EVENLY OVER THE SYRUP FILLING AND BAKES THE PIE IMMEDIATELY.

BETTY'S AMISH VANILLA PIE

Makes a 23cm (9in) pie, to serve 8–10
PASTRY:
185g (6¹/₂oz) plain flour
¹/₄ teaspoon salt
60g (2oz) lard or white vegetable fat, chilled and
    diced
30g (1oz) butter, chilled and diced
2–3 tablespoons icy water

FILLING:
455ml (16fl oz) water
100g (3¹/₂oz) caster sugar
2 tablespoons plain flour
340g (12oz) black treacle or molasses
1 egg, beaten
1 teaspoon pure vanilla essence

CRUMB TOPPING:
140g (5oz) plain flour
100g (3¹/₂oz) caster sugar
60g (2oz) butter, chilled and diced
¹/₄ teaspoon bicarbonate of soda
¹/₄ teaspoon cream of tartar

a 23cm (9in) pie dish, about 4cm (1¹/₂in) deep,
    or loose-based flan tin

Preheat the oven to 190C (375F, Gas 5).

Make the pastry dough, line the pie dish and part-bake the case as for Shoo Fly Pie (see page 183). Leave to cool.

To make the filling, heat the water in a saucepan over moderate heat until it is fairly hot but nowhere near boiling. Mix the sugar with the flour and whisk into the hot water. Whisk in the treacle. As soon as it has melted and the mixture is smooth, whisk in the egg. Continue whisking until the mixture thickens – it should barely come to a simmer and must not boil. Remove from the heat and leave to cool before stirring in the vanilla.

To make the crumb topping, put all the ingredients into a mixing bowl and rub between your fingertips until the mixture resembles fine crumbs.

Pour the filling into the cooled pie case, and sprinkle the top evenly with the crumb topping. Bake for 10 minutes, then reduce the oven temperature to 180C (350F, Gas 4) and bake for a further 30 minutes or until the centre of the filling is firm when the pie dish is gently shaken. Serve at room temperature.

An Amish horse and buggy in Lancaster County, Pennsylvania.

RIGHT Shoo Fly Pie and an uncut Amish Vanilla Pie.

STEPHEN BULL'S PECAN BUTTER TART

INGREDIENTS

Makes a 25.5cm (10in) tart, to serve up
  to 16
PASTRY:
230g (8oz) plain flour
a pinch of salt
30g (1oz) caster sugar
155g (5¹/₂oz) unsalted butter, chilled and diced
1 egg yolk, size 2, mixed with 1 tablespoon icy
  water

FILLING:
280g (10oz) dark muscovado sugar
230g (8oz) unsalted butter
170g (6oz) maple syrup
170g (6oz) golden syrup
5 eggs, size 2
1 teaspoon pure vanilla essence
170g (6oz) raisins
500g (1lb 2oz) pecans, roughly chopped

a 25.5cm (10in) loose-based deep flan tin or
  springclip tin

ABOVE A piece of wonderful Pecan Butter Tart.

TOP RIGHT Stephen Bull and his Pecan Butter
Tart in the Fulham Road restaurant.

I first tasted this most wonderful of traditional butter-rich pecan pies at Vivian's, our local deli in Richmond, Surrey. Vivian is an old friend of the chef and restaurateur, Stephen Bull, who once had a restaurant nearby and now has three in London – Fulham Road, the restaurant in Blandford Street, and The Bistro in St John Street. I decided to take the bull by the horns, as it were, and ask for the recipe. It requires a lot of expensive nuts, but the pie is very large and cuts into 16 slices.

Make the pastry dough by hand (see page 132) or in a food processor: sift the flour, salt and sugar into the processor bowl, add the diced butter and process until the mixture resembles fine crumbs. With the machine running, add the egg and water mixture through the feed tube. Run the machine until the dough comes together in a ball. It should be soft but not sticky. If this has not happened after a minute and there are dry crumbs, add more water, a teaspoon at a time. Wrap and chill for 15 minutes.

Preheat the oven to 200C (400F, Gas 6).

On a floured work surface, roll out the dough to a round about 33cm (13in) in diameter and use to line the tin. Prick the bottom of the pastry case all over with a fork, then chill for 10 minutes. Bake the pastry case blind (see page 158), then leave to cool while making the filling. Reduce the oven temperature to 150C (300F, Gas 2).

Put the sugar, butter and both syrups into a large saucepan and bring to the boil. Cook over moderate heat for 5 minutes, stirring frequently to prevent sticking, then remove from the heat and set aside. Put the eggs into a large bowl and beat well, then stir in the vanilla essence, the raisins and, finally, the nuts. When thoroughly blended, add the syrup mixture and mix well.

Pour the filling into the baked pastry case and bake for 1 hour or until the filling is fairly firm to the touch. Allow to cool, and serve with cream or vanilla ice-cream.

DIANE'S CHOCOLATE PECAN PIE

INGREDIENTS

Makes a 23cm (9in) pie, to serve 8
PASTRY:
140g (5oz) plain flour
$^1/_2$ teaspoon salt
85g (3oz) fat (see recipe), chilled and diced if using
    butter or lard
2-3 tablespoons icy water

FILLING:
110g (4oz) margarine or butter, melted
35g (1$^1/_4$oz) plain flour
30g (1oz) cocoa powder
200g (7oz) caster sugar
$^1/_4$ teaspoon pure vanilla essence
2 eggs, beaten
100g (3$^1/_2$oz) pecan halves

TO FINISH:
60g (2oz) pecan halves

a 23cm (9in) pie dish, about 4cm (1$^1/_2$in) deep,
    or loose-based flan tin

Diane Dorsey makes light, melt-in-the-mouth pastry for her pecan pie.

James Swink of Young's Pecans in North Carolina recommended that we visit the best pecan pie baker he knew — Diane Dorsey. Diane was very matter of fact about her wonderful, unusual pecan pie, the recipe for which is much sought after locally. Diane said she made it up by combining her favourite fudge and traditional pecan pie recipes. The result is like a very nutty brownie in a pastry case. Diane makes her pastry with shortening, but you can use butter, lard, margarine or white vegetable fat instead.

In South Carolina, much of the pecan crop comes from yard, or back garden, trees rather than commercial orchards.

Preheat the oven to 180C (350F, Gas 4).

To make the pastry dough, put the flour and salt into a mixing bowl and add the fat. If using shortening, mix it into the flour with a spoon or round-bladed knife; hard fats should be rubbed in with your fingertips until the mixture resembles fine crumbs. Then add the water and mix, using your hands or a round-bladed knife, to make a soft but not sticky dough. Knead very gently until the dough just comes together.

Turn the dough on to a lightly floured work surface. Roll out fairly thinly into a round about 30.5cm (12in) in diameter. Rather than roll up the dough around the rolling pin, Diane uses this method: fold the dough in half and in half again, into quarters, and lift it into the pie dish. Unfold the dough and press it gently on to the bottom and sides to line the dish completely. Decorate the pastry rim by pressing down all around with the back of a fork, then cut off any excess dough. Leave in a cool place – not the fridge – while preparing the filling.

Mix the melted fat with the flour using a metal or wooden spoon; don't worry if the mixture looks slightly lumpy. Add the cocoa and mix well. Stir in the sugar, then the vanilla and, finally, the eggs. When thoroughly blended, stir in the pecans.

Pour the filling into the pastry case. Decorate with the extra nuts. Bake for 25 minutes or until the filling feels just firm to the touch. Leave to cool completely, and serve at room temperature.

ABOVE At Young's Pecans, the nuts are graded for size and then checked for damage before shelling.

RIGHT Chocolate Pecan Pie, combining the best of traditional pecan pies with chocolate fudge.

APPLE ALMOND CREAM PIE

Makes a 23cm (9in) pie, to serve 8
PASTRY:
230g (8oz) plain flour
a pinch of salt
60g (2oz) unsalted butter, chilled and diced
60g (2oz) lard or white vegetable fat, chilled and diced
2–3 tablespoons icy water to bind

ALMOND CREAM:
230g (8oz) almond paste (marzipan), crumbled
110g (4oz) unsalted butter, at room temperature, diced
2 tablespoons plain flour
2 eggs, beaten

TOPPING:
4 large, tart eating apples
1 tablespoon lemon juice
2 tablespoons caster sugar

a 23cm (9in) metal pie plate or dish, about 4cm (1¹/₂in) deep

ABOVE The Isaac Randall House in Freeport, Maine, home of the Friedlanders.

TOP RIGHT (from left to right): Apple Almond Cream Pie, Bayberry Bread, Granny Glyn's Lemon Loaf (recipes for the breads are on pages 100–101).

OPPOSITE Jim Friedlander takes a freshly baked Apple Almond Cream Pie from the oven.

This is one of the best apple pies I have ever tasted. The recipe comes from Jim Friedlander of Freeport, Maine (also see pages 100-101). It is much easier to make than it first appears, though a food processor is essential. You also need good, tart eating apples such as Granny Smiths — Bramley apples become too fluffy and juicy during cooking.

Preheat the oven to 230C (450F, Gas 8) .

Make the pastry dough by hand (see page 132) or in the food processor: put the flour, salt and fats into the processor bowl and process until the mixture looks like fine crumbs. With the motor running, slowly pour in 2 tablespoons of the water through the feed tube. If the dough has not come together to form a ball within a minute, gradually add more water, to make a soft but not sticky dough.

Turn the dough on to a lightly floured work surface. Cut off a third of the dough; wrap and chill the larger portion. Roll out the smaller piece to a round about 30.5cm (12in) in diameter and use to line the pie plate. Let the excess dough hang over the rim. Put on one side.

Now prepare the almond cream. Put the almond paste and butter into the bowl of the food processor and process until smooth. Add the flour and the eggs and process once more, until the mixture is smooth, creamy and thoroughly blended.

Peel, halve and core the apples, then cut into slices 1cm (³/₈in) thick. Cut each slice crosswise into three. Put the apples in a bowl and toss with the lemon juice and sugar.

Spoon the almond cream mixture into the bottom of the pastry case, then cover with the apples, mounding them slightly in the centre. Roll out the remaining dough to a round about 28cm (11in) in diameter to make the lid. Dampen the rim of the pastry case, then cover the pie with the pastry lid. Press the edges together to seal firmly. Using a sharp knife, cut off the excess dough, then cut 6 slits in the pastry lid.

Put the pie in the preheated oven, then immediately reduce the oven temperature to 190C (375F, Gas 5). Bake for 45–50 minutes or until golden brown, then sprinkle with a little sugar and leave to cool. Serve warm or at room temperature.

A LIST OF SUPPLIERS

FLOUR
Mike Thurlow
Letheringsett Mill
Holt, Norfolk NR25 7YD
Tel: 01263 713153
Shop, and will also send goods by mail order.

BAKING TINS
Alan Silverwood Ltd
Ledsam Street Works
Birmingham B16 8DN
Tel: 0121 454 3571/2
Telephone for stockists; will also send goods by mail order.

KITCHEN EQUIPMENT
The Kitchenware Company
36 Hill Street
Richmond, Surrey TW9 1TW
Tel: 0181 948 7785
Will send goods by mail order, and also offer advice on baking tins.

David Mellor
4 Sloane Square
London SW1 8EE
Tel: 0171 730 4259
Will send goods by mail order (telephone for catalogue) and also offer advice on baking tins.

Divertimenti
45–47 Wigmore Street
London W1H 9LE
Tel: 0171 935 0689
Will send goods by mail order (telephone for catalogue) and also offer advice on baking tins.

The Kitchen Range
162 High Street
Beckenham, Kent BR3 1EW
Tel: 0181 663 6323
Will send goods by mail order, and also offer advice on baking tins.

Buyers & Sellers
120 Ladbroke Grove
London W10 5NE
Tel: 0171 229 1947
Nationwide delivery, and also offer advice on ovens and cookers.

Lakeland Plastics Ltd
Alexandra Buildings
Windermere, Cumbria LA23 1BQ
Tel: 01539 88200
Shop, and will also send goods by mail order (telephone for catalogue).

ACKNOWLEDGEMENTS

Linda Collister and Anthony Blake would like to thank the following people and companies:

IN THE UNITED STATES:
Lucinda Hampton (Pennsylvania Dutch Visitors Bureau), Dottie and Andy Hess, Betty and Abe Groff, Dee Dee and Jack Meyer, Will and Annette Hertz, Rosemary Underdahl, Jim Friedlander, Lois and Ezia Lamdin, Caroll Boltin, and at Young's Pecans, Florence, South Carolina, James Swink, Helen Watts, Diane Dorsey, Shawn Price and Mac Davenport.

IN FRANCE:
Kate and John Barber, Jean-Jacques Bernachon and Jean-Pierre St Martin.

IN GREAT BRITAIN:
Joy Skipper, Barbara Levy, Norma MacMillan, Paul Welti, Sharon Turner and Yvonne Jenkins, Stephen Bull, Marc and Max Renzland, Brigitte Friis, Zeynep Stromfelt, Katie Stewart, Sallie Morris, Alan Hertz, Michael Sealey, Rena Salaman, Betty Charlton, Jean Bush, Alice Portnoy at Neff and Sheila Rossen.

IN GERMANY:
Nürnberg Tourist Office.

FOR PHOTOGRAPHY:
Uli Hintner at Leica Cameras.
for crockery and cutlery: Villeroy and Boch; for equipment: The Kitchenware Company; for kitchen appliances: Neff, Braun, Kenwood, Magimix.

INDEX

Page numbers in *italic* refer to the illustrations